Spiritual Awakening

A guide to spiritual life in congregations

John Ackerman

An Alban Institute Publication

The Publications Program of The Alban Institute is assisted by a grant from Trinity Church, New York City.

Library of Congress Catalog Number 94-78335
ISBN #1-56699-135-8

CONTENTS

ACKNOWLEDGMENTS

I want to thank the myriads of people, starting with my mother, who nurured my awareness of God. These include my spiritual directors over twenty years. Mary Sharon Riley, rc, now in Rome, continued to ask me if I had spoken to God and how God had responded. Her questions have now become mine. There were the developers and leaders of Beginning Again, the spiritual formation course outlined in the first part of this book: Leigh Bailey, Jim Bowe, Dolores Costello, and Sheila Crombie.

My spiritual directors' supervision group has been very helpful; I thank especially Marilyn Beckstrom and Mark Scannell. My parish has been generous in encouraging me and trying new things. One parish leader, Angi Hooker, read this material several times.

My consultant, Dr. Richard Fowler, tried to straighten out my thinking on adult development, and Carol Pierce approved my using some material on male-female differences. Carol has written many books on male-female differences. Carolyn Osiek, teacher and author at the Catholic Theological Union in Chicago, approved my using material she developed on temperament and surrender. And Linda Berens gave permission to adapt some of her temperament material. She has researched and written extensively about the application of psychological temperament to work. From a lay Roman Catholic background, Vern Paul provided good advice, particularly about story telling. A professor at Bethel Seminary. Jeannette Bakke, provided an evangelical point of view, and Lindsay Biddle, feminist friend, took time to give me her feedback.

I also thank the editor of The Alban Institute, Celia Hahn, who focused my thinking about the parish as a whole. She asked me to write not only about individual spiritual growth, but also about what can be done to encourage corporate spirituality in a parish setting. And Evelyn Bence painstakingly edited and reedited and tried to get this clear.

INTRODUCTION

Your eyes are windows into your body. If you open your eyes wide in wonder and belief, your body fills up with light. If you live squinty-eyed in greed and distrust, your body is a dank cellar.
—Matthew 6:22 (TM)

Give your entire attention to what God is doing right now.
—Matthew 6:33 (TM)

This book is written to help people wake up to the presence of God. How can we learn to listen to and see God at work in our lives?

I love to talk about spiritual *awakening*. Why? I'm convinced that everyone has some experience of God, even if it's an awareness of God's absence. Yet many people aren't able to articulate this longing for beauty or love or truth or a spiritual "home"—until they are encouraged to identify it.

Awakening—the word has both traditional and contemporary overtones. Beginning in the eighteenth century, philosophers of the Enlightenment denied the need for God and turned their trust to materialism and reason. Yet this same period of history fostered great awakenings of the Spirit: the Great Awakening in New England, Pietism in Germany, and Wesley's evangelical revivals in England. And today the phrase *spiritual awakening* is increasingly heard in mainline, Roman Catholic, and evangelical circles—even outside the organized church. It refers to a hunger evident in our culture.

What Are People Searching For?

The reality of God. People are yearning for and finding what women and
men found in the Great Awakening: a vital personal relationship with
the living God. Too often people do not find this in their local parishes.
The normal parish may focus on one style of spirituality, such as Cursillo,
prayer groups, or social action, but few encourage a variety of spiritual
approaches that suit the temperamental needs of a wide range of people.

Community, not hierarchy. People want to find God in the company of other seekers, often in an informal setting that includes people of
all ages.

Empowerment to find God. People need to be empowered to find
their own pathway to God. For too long churches have been more concerned with running programs than with helping their parishioners find
and follow the direction of God. Our people need specific help for their
personal spiritual growth. They need to talk about how they can find
God's call in their jobs and relationships.

An inclusive spirituality. People are looking for a broad, inclusive
approach to spirituality that is more than "Jesus and me." Yes, they want
a close intimacy with God, but increasingly people want transparent relationships with their spouses and a few close friends. They also desire a
theological stance that is open to people of other religions, evangelism
that has more to do with "sharing their stories" than with clobbering
people over the head.

Overview of the Book

This book is based on a practical approach like that found in *The Spiritual Exercises of Ignatius of Loyola.* It is more like a laboratory course
than a lecture. It is more like putting on a play than reading about plays.
It is like being married, or at least dating, rather than exploring theories
of relationships.

Part one of this book outlines an eight-week Beginning Again
course I have developed and used to encourage spiritual awakening in a
variety of settings: with individuals, in small groups, and in whole parishes; in a twelve-step set-up, in mainline churches, with Roman Catholic
teachers, and with evangelical clergy.

The churchwide model or pattern I used came from an evangelical program produced by the Chapel of the Air. They had developed a partial systems approach, combining worship and small groups and individual work.

I revised the Beginning Again material for a full-credit course in a doctor of ministry program at Bethel Seminary. Teaching clergy for three years and my work with clergy support groups have stimulated the material in the second part of the book.

Part two might be called a systems approach to spiritual formation and development. It is designed for parish leaders—cleric and lay who work in the arena of spiritual guidance with people of all temperaments.

My suggestions for congregations bolster Eugene Peterson's comment:

> The paradigm shift that I am after is from pastor as program director to pastor as spiritual director. . . . This is not the formulation of something new but the recovery of something original.[1]

My approach gives principles of spiritual guidance and direction for the congregational setting.

Part three of the book gives a few practical specifics for leaders.

Targeted Readers

I have written this book for three kinds of readers:

Clergy in a parish setting. When I've told pastors about this book-writing project, I've sensed their desire for a case-study or story-telling approach rather than a how–to manual. They want to be able to adapt my material to suit their congregational needs. I do not have a one-size-fits-all approach. What you'll find here is an attitudinal foundation that will help a wide variety of people discover what God is doing in their parish and person.

Seminarians. At Union Seminary in New York City, I was intellectually prepared for ministry. But there I was not touched spiritually except by one man, James Muilenburg, who introduced us to the personalities and spirituality of the Old Testament. Still, no one told me how I could find the God of Abraham, Isaac, and Jacob.

I spent one year of seminary in Scotland. I there learned something of the life of the Spirit when I worked on an evangelism campaign and heard evangelical teaching from several professors. Still, no one talked about prayer; no one encouraged us in spiritual formation. Seminarians talked *about* God, not *with* God.

In seminary there is incredible pressure to read about religion, learn ideas, practice the profession. More and more seminary students are taking courses in spiritual formation, but as a rule neither they nor their teachers have much parish experience in guiding people individually and in groups.

Lay leaders. One trained, lay spiritual director recently explained his situation. His Roman Catholic parish has three spiritual directors and ten thousand parishioners. Many people want to join spiritual growth groups, but how can the church train laypeople to lead the groups? What material might they use? I have written this book with this scenario in mind. Actually, the book was partly written by laypeople who have helped me develop and lead the Beginning Again course.

Definitions

To help readers understand where I'm coming from, I offer the following explanation of my style and terms frequently used.

Inclusive language. I have not altered quoted texts to make them gender inclusive. In my own text, I have tried to include both male and female experience.

Holy Spirit. By *Spirit* I mean the Holy Spirit, the Lord, the Giver of life, who spoke through the prophets and uniquely in Jesus Christ. The Spirit of God may be discerned in our individual and corporate experience because the Spirit confirms the truth of the gospel, leads us to service for others, and advances the relationship we have with Jesus Christ.

Spirit. I use the lower-cased spirit to refer to the human spirit and soul—that interweaving of God and person within. An organization or group might also have a (lower-cased) spirit. A person or organization may have a good or a destructive spirit or angel.

Spirituality. In this sense, generic *spirituality* refers to the relationships everyone has with God, neighbor, and self. These relationships may be destructive or constructive, conscious or subconscious.

Christian spirituality is a specific quality of relationship-loving God, neighbor, and self and receiving love and grace. Perhaps the fullest expression of Christian spirituality in the New Testament is in Paul's prayer that the Ephesians be:

strengthened in your inner being with power through his Spirit, and that Christ may dwell in your hearts through faith, as you are being rooted and grounded in love . . . and [that you] know the love of Christ that surpasses knowledge, so that you may be filled with all the fullness of God (Eph. 3:16-19).

Spirituality is the heart attitude behind formal belief and practice. I particularly like one definition:

Spirituality consists not in becoming more and more responsible in the fulfillment of a duty, but in becoming more and more faithful in a love relationship . . . not so much a question of running up a steep hill . . . as it is a letting go, . . . falling backward in trust, believing that we will be caught up in loving protective arms.[2]

I also see Christian spirituality as becoming part of a mutual, interpersonal community, based on the pattern of the Trinity. This relationship is not private, rather it connects me with the universal love of God and a specific group of people—family, neighbors, my congregation, and the poor.

Religion. In using this word I refer to the manifest buildings, organizations, liturgies, theologies, prayers, beliefs, and hopes that may or may not support an active Christian spirituality. Optimists think that religion and spirituality are the same thing. Pessimists doubt that they ever overlap. At best, the Christian religion is the framework for the spiritual life.

At the beginning of part two I give further definitions for three forms of spiritual guidance.

I've given considerable attention to these definitions; if my usage of the terms still confuses you, try what a Shakespeare scholar recommended for attending Shakespeare plays: Get centered; don't fight the strange language. After a while your ear does the translation for you.

In the Parish: Beginning Again

My tenure at Bryn Mawr Presbyterian Church has opened into blessings I never expected. When I arrived in 1989, the small church was on the verge of closing. Since I had come from a very large church and represented Bryn Mawr's "last hope," parishioners were willing to try almost anything I suggested. Many of the lay leaders were conservative theologically. The parishioners, most past retirement age, had a generous attitude toward me and other new people. They were like grandparents who are so glad to welcome home the younger generations that they overlook some differences in style. I was like the new son, the other newcomers were treated like the grandchildren, and we were all accepted into the family.

Having previously learned some hard lessons about pushing my own agenda, this time, I tried to listen to the spirit of the parish and to what the Spirit of God was saying. One young man said we were like Lake Wobegon of "A Prairie Home Companion" fame. Right! I changed my leadership style to match the community.

Families were attracted by our informality, the small-town character, the down-to-earth preaching. As newer families moved into leadership, I started to ask questions: Who were we, and what direction should we go in? As we'd grown we'd become such a diverse group. What could we agree on? What kind of growth were we interested in?

We hired a consultant to help us write a mission statement, and we discovered that encouraging spiritual growth was one of our major goals. We drew pictures of where we perceived God in our life together and then translated these into a mission statement.

One part of the statement shocked me: "developing personal relationships with God." This had not been a major priority in any church

I'd served. The statement seemed too good to be true. Could they be serious? Was it just a pious phrase to please me? I didn't ask the questions for long.

After the church leaders articulated spiritual awakening or growth as a goal, they decided to ask people where they were in their priorities and spiritual practices. We stopped evaluating the bottom line in terms of numbers of people or dollars and started to wonder how we could tell if people were growing spiritually. I developed a questionnaire that asks about loving God, neighbor, and self and the practices that help with this awareness or awakening.

We also started the eight-week Beginning Again program. With the assistance of lay program designers, I had already developed this program over three years and led it with lay leaders in various parishes. The heart of the program was encouraging laypeople to tell their stories of noticing God's presence in their lives and finding a practice that fit them for regularly seeking God.

We introduced this program to the congregation on three levels: (1) In Sunday worship service I preached on the theme of the week. Before and during the service, parishioners told their own stories. (2) In weekly small-group meetings people told their stories; meetings often included meditative prayer. About half of the congregation signed up for these groups. (3) Take-home written material suggested daily practices.

As a result of this church-wide approach, the whole church grew increasingly open to telling stories and talking about personal experiences of God. A different kind of community developed.

The first time we ran a new-member class after the program, a young woman who led the get-acquainted time told her story of God in her life and invited the new members to do so if they wished. I was amazed because this woman hadn't been in a small group. She had just picked up the storytelling from the group culture!

The communal attitude of our congregation is radically different from most churches I know about. Some Roman Catholics would call us a base community. Some evangelicals would think of us as an expanded small group. I think of us as being like the small-town church I grew up in, but we are more open to share where we are in our search for God.

I see clear evidence that more parishioners are able to see their work as being connected to God's call. Mary, for instance, came to church looking for "something more" besides preaching, music, and children's programs.

Mary's religious practice was conventional and sporadic. She had trouble sorting out what in her experience was from God. She believed in God who was "out there" in scripture and at church, but what about the longings in her life? Were they from God? She listened to me talk about God in my life story, but it was a big shift for her to find this presence of God within herself.

In the context of a small group Mary started to open up. The leaders told their stories. One man had been divorced and found God (or been found by God) in the midst of the pain. Mary began to look back through her pain as well. She started writing her story. What made her feel "connected"? She liked the meditative prayer at the beginning of the group meetings. It touched her heart and imagination as well as her mind. She told her story, felt affirmed, and found support for sifting out her experiences, for finding God's call outside and inside her. Instead of living out a surface-level, seemingly perfect "Barbie and Ken" marriage, she chose to work through some marital differences and develop more depth in the relationship.

She started to pray early in the morning, before the rest of her family got up. She meditated. She discovered some dark aspects of her life and some gifts that she had taken for granted. As she journaled about her pain, she felt more in touch with her real self; God seemed more real.

Your story will be different from Mary's, but I see the awakening as being much the same for everyone: learning to recognize God's hand and voice in one's life because one has shared the process with others, responding in prayer, meditation, and love.

This pattern was evident in the life of Ignatius of Loyola:

> For Ignatius, finding God in all things is what life is all about . . .
> Finding God in the present moment, feeling or option was almost
> instantaneous in his mature years because the central "feel" or
> "bent" of his being had been grasped by God. . . .
> Thus discernment of spirits became a daily very practical
> living in the art of loving God with his whole heart, whole body,
> and whole strength. Every moment of life was loving (finding) God
> in the existential situation in a deep quiet, peace, and joy.[1]

That capsulizes the goal I have for every member of our church—and for you and your friends: learning to recognize God's hand and voice in every aspect of life.

My great joy, Lord, is to praise you;
    I will sing and awaken the dawn.
Wake up, my soul; wake up,
    Music in the depths of my heart (Ps. 57:8–9).[2]

CHAPTER 1

Telling Your Story

God loves stories: that's why he created us!
—Elie Wiesel

Listen to your life. See it for the fathomless mystery that it is. In the boredom and the pain of it no less than the excitement and gladness: touch, taste, smell your way to the holy and hidden heart of it because in the last analysis all moments are key moments, and life itself is grace.[1]
—Frederick Buechner

I love the Easter story of the two disciples on the Emmaus road. They didn't know the risen Lord was walking beside them. But then, after breaking bread, "Their eyes were opened, and they recognized him" (Luke 24:31).

How do we recognize God in our lives? By paying attention to our own stories and being receptive to grace. Stories help us pay attention to our experience of God, and until we know God, how can we love God?

As children many of us had a natural sense of God. In time the predominant culture may have trained us to see things through a lens tainted by materialism and secularism. But God is there. We just have to recognize the presence of the Spirit.

Adults may be inspired to recognize the presence of God in their lives by hearing others tell their stories. Biographies of saints may shine light on our own lives. But such stories often do not speak to our experience. At one time I used many literary or dramatic sermon illustrations, but too many people could not identify with the hero or heroine.

I now pepper my sermons with stories about ordinary people. Including a variety of stories— about women, minorities, people of other faith groups—can help break down prejudices and build bridges. Didn't Jesus make heroines of a Samaritan woman and a poor widow—social outcasts? But I also tell and encourage others to tell stories of people whose life patterns are very similar to those of my parishioners.

A number of young adults related well to another young adult who told her experience of the transcendent. I sensed a new openness to and awareness of the Spirit. *You mean that weird experience I had.... It was okay?*

What might hold people back from telling their stories—or seeing God at work in their lives?

Some people, often "cradle evangelicals," have stereotypical expectations of the "normal" religious experience. They may have desperately prayed to "be saved" and yet never have felt any assurance of that salvation. Thinking they've never measured up to the norm, they assume God is not at work in their lives. To these people I point out a pattern of Jesus' teaching: The "outsiders" of his day were often closer to the kingdom than those who thought they were inside. In Matthew 7:21 he says, "Not everyone who says to me, 'Lord, Lord,' will enter the kingdom of heaven, but only the one who does the will of my Father in heaven."

Some people are afraid that their stories may be too simple to share. And yet, like the surprising words of wisdom uttered by a young child, a simple, transparent story has a charm that can powerfully touch others. And consider that the Gospels are full of Jesus' "simple" stories; much of the Old Testament is the story of a people.

Stories have great power to communicate the reality of God. Theology may help some; music may touch the hearts of others, but stories and ritual can speak to almost everyone at every level of development.

And the power of a personal story affects the teller and the hearer. I frequently ask parishioners to tell their stories—in small groups and privately. As the tale unfolds, I almost always sense that I am on holy ground, that I should take off my shoes and bow in reverence. And as I verbally reflect on themes I've heard in their stories, the storytellers are almost universally appreciative and grateful.

How can we encourage others to tell their stories?

We often feel safest talking about childhood memories. It's easier to "let out" some part of the past than to explain the present. In a group I model this by relating my earliest memories, for example:

My first specific spiritual and religious memory is going to church with my mother and father. I was bored most of the time, but the church atmosphere caught my attention—especially during communion. The congregation was like an extended family to me. And these significant adults were unusually quiet during this ritual. Something holy was here. I looked at the stained glass windows, listned to the music, and heard the liturgical words over and over. In the communion service, the world, the community, the family, and myself—all was at peace.

Later, at a boarding school, I went to communion, maybe because I felt at home there; it connected me to the home and hometown I had left behind.

Sometimes people respond well to a different type of question: Where did you first feel connected—at home in the universe? My own response would be:

In the bath tub. In the cold winters of upstate New York, the tub was warm and secure. I was free from the restraint of clothing; I could play with the soap and splash with the rubber ducks. A few minutes in a warm bath still restores my sense of well-being.

After hearing that portion of my story, one keen listener asked, "And where else have you found God in water?" Her question—on top of the one I'd originally asked—sent me down a new "memory lane" that I wouldn't have found if I had articulated my spiritual journey only in terms of religious words or conscious contact with God. I remembered boyhood visits to the beach, swimming holes, baptisms—secular and holy all together.

Some reluctant story tellers respond to another question: In what season of your life did you feel most restless, meaningless, or directionless? Augustine said, "Our hearts are restless until we find our rest in Thee." Restlessness can force us to reach out for spiritual help. I mention highlights of my loneliness as an adolescent—how I reached out to God in the communion service and in choir singing. In my sophomore year in college, I didn't really believe in God, yet in my desolation I reached out and prayed.

How did you experience the Mystery as a child, as an adolescent, and now as an adult? Was it in relationships with those you love?

Through tragedies and the trauma of survival? Did you hear the Spirit in a sermon or lecture?

Is the Mystery connected with Beauty? Again I quote Augustine, who said, "Late have I loved Thee, o Beauty ever ancient, ever new." Some people find God in the out-of-doors. The mountains do it for me. In my office I have hung a photograph of the Alps, to remind me of the sense of awe I experienced there. Native Americans around Glacier Park believe that the spirits live in the mountains. It's easy for me to understand why.

Others find God in a call to responsibility or duty or in sacrifice to a greater good. On this count I think of the great challenge of Abraham Lincoln's Gettysburg Address: to be "dedicated to the great task remaining before us...."

As we tell—and especially as we write down—the history of our experience of God, we can more easily see that, and how, God has been there with us and in us.

Looking at one's own life is similar to studying the Bible. Having a big picture of God's activity down through the ages can reveal God's work and word in a particular biblical chapter. Similarly, having a sense of the big sweep of God's work in our lives enlightens specific moments of grace that God gives us every day.

But a warning: We need to move past one experience, past our first understanding of God's work in our lives. Samuel Miller warns against two extremes:

> Never to put your finger down to affirm God's presence in this place is to live forever outside of His kingdom; to put it down and never move it is to mistake a souvenir for God. A healthy soul is bold enough to affirm God in the midst of temporal imperfections, and strong enough to follow Him in the pilgrimage of moving time.[2]

As we identify God in the reality of our lives, we need to be open to God's movement in new areas.

The stories of the Bible can always be used to spur, question, illuminate, and confront our own stories. I find that people who are able to recognize God in their own stories are better able to recognize God in the "Master Story," to use a phrase of John Shea, a Catholic priest who specializes in "storytelling." And the reverse is true: As people recognize God in the Bible, they can often see where God is acting in their lives.

Are there parallels between your story and that of the Bible? As
preparation for his joining the church, I asked a Hmong refugee to write
down his story and the history of his people. I was impressed with his
insights into being a stranger in a foreign land. When I summarized for
him the stories of aliens Abraham and Joseph, he nodded knowingly.
When I mentioned Jesus' suffering, he nodded vigorously. When I told
him about the Spirit, he told me about his animist understanding of the
spirits. We concluded that God was at work in both traditions.

I close these reflections on "Telling Your Story" with a quote I
found on an old sheet of paper. The author is credited as Bernard
Phillips; no other source is given. Whoever or wherever Mr. Phillips
may be, I trust he will appreciate a new generation of readers contem-
plating his wisdom:

> There are many who look to psychology or psychotherapy or to
> spiritual writing for answers, and this is all right up to a point, but
> pushed too far it becomes an escape from one's self, from one's
> own reality. If you keep asking, "How shall I do it?" you are not
> meeting your own life situation. Only your own life can teach you
> how it is to be lived. If we turn to psychology or to religion because
> we are afraid to face our own life, to sweat and toil and to shed tears
> and to learn to love in the context of your own life situation, then
> psychology and religion have become obstacles to reality. Since
> this is what happens to most people, it can perhaps be said paradoxi-
> cally that the greatest obstacle to self–understanding is psychology,
> and the greatest obstacle to spirituality is religion. One must never
> approach these as forms of knowledge which exempt one from the
> necessity of actually living and learning from life itself or from God
> in your life.

Notes for Leaders

•   *Beginning Again sessions.* For small groups meeting for Beginning
Again sessions, I spend two weeks on this topic. The first week is an introduction of the whole series. We get acquainted, and the leader gives
guidelines for the weeks ahead. Group guidelines include confidentiality
and commitment, putting attendance before social responsibilities.

I like to start with a guided meditation: Remember where God became more than an empty word for you. We ask participants to talk about this to one other person and with the group, if people are willing.

The group leader tells his or her own story. Knowing it is not appropriate to reveal "everything" with a church group, I model story telling in the middle range of intimacy—neither superficial nor revealing the deepest secrets. Your parish, like ours, may be fortunate to include people active in twelve-step programs who are practiced in speaking publicly at this middle range of self-revelation. Their ease tends to open others up.

At the beginning of the storytelling, I encourage three kinds of responses that relate profound respect, as if the listener were standing on holy ground: (1) "Thank you," "Wow," or some appreciative noise. (2) Respectful questions, such as, "Could you tell me what it felt like when you were baptized?" Some people need help to be specific. (3) Verbalized reflection that points out perceived patterns, such as, "As I listened, I heard a pattern—your being open to God as a child, then going through a long dry spell, and now being receptive again. Is that right?"

A weekly Beginning Again format follows this pattern: (1) Check-in: How are you and what is God up to in your life? (2) Meditation: Usually I connect it to the subject matter at hand. (3) Presentation and discussion of the subject. (4) One participant tells his story; let people respond— noting what struck them or asking one question about the "growing edge." (5) Closing. Standing, holding hands, and saying the Lord's Prayer or the Serenity Prayer. People sometimes tell one thing they heard and want to remember or one thing they are grateful for.

At the end of the first session I hand out the "Guidelines for Writing and Telling Your Story" found at the end of this chapter. I ask people to write their stories before session 2 (in chapter 2). An alternate approach would be to have people spend an hour to ninety minutes of session 1 or 2 writing their stories.

In session 2 we have participants tell their stories, paraphrasing what they've written. You may prefer to have the stories told one or two per session, throughout the whole course series.

As people tell their stories, clergy, especially, may be tempted to jump in with advice or a story of their own. But I would discourage advice giving, unless specifically requested, and telling one's own tale, which is often "off base" and not particularly helpful.

   •   *Committee meetings.* When members of church groups meeting around potentially divisive subjects tell their stories, the win-lose atmosphere tends to dissipate.

At a recent meeting of the finance committee, I suggested that we each tell something of what we learned about money as we were growing up. I told my own vignette and others followed. This allowed us to start the meeting with an appreciation for others' financial backgrounds.

- *Teaching church leaders.* When teaching church leaders to listen well, I divide the group up into threes. One is the storyteller. One is the listener. The third is the observer. For half an hour, the storyteller talks. The listener occasionally makes reflective comments or asks questions. It takes skill to listen deeply and articulate comments and questions that deepen the speaker's awareness. Then the observer leads the evaluation process: The story teller and listener reflect on the process, then the observer provides feedback. Did the listener reflect what was most significant? What did the observer hear—or see in body language? In what ways did the observer note the presence of the Spirit?

- *With skilled listeners.* In my monthly support group of spiritual directors, we have one director reflectively listen to a directee for fifteen minutes, commenting and asking questions in front of the whole group. The topic at hand: My work with this one person. The emphasis is never on how to fix the directee, but on what the Spirit is doing in the director-presenter. Where did the director-presenter hear well? Where not? What distortion, if any, does the group pick up? Where was the director not responsive to the Spirit?

HANDOUT

Guidelines for Writing and Telling Your Story

As you prayerfully remember your holy history, consider these questions. Some—not all— might bring to mind memories and patterns of God's work in your life.

1.   What was the spirituality and religion of your parents and grandparents? What overt messages did you receive? What unspoken messages? What do you want to inherit, and what do you want to leave behind?

2.   Try to separate your parents' experience and your childhood teaching and practice from the God who greets you now.

3.   How did you experience God as a child? How do you experience God now? How do you know what the character of God is like? By what standard (scripture, church, your experience) can you measure an experience to determine whether or not it's of God?

4.   Have you ever turned over your life to the care of God?

5.   How do you distinguish the leading of God from your willfulness? Can you step back and detach yourself from the destructive voices within you?

6.   How do you get in touch with your powerlessness? Does it cause you to withdraw and cut yourself off from others and God or does it draw you to others and God?

7.   How have you sensed the Holy Mystery, truth, or beauty that took your breath away?

8.   Where have you felt deeply connected or "at home"? Has this been in action or in being still?

HANDOUT continued

9.   Consider the pain or suffering in your life, the times when God has seemed absent.

10. What brings you to this new adventure-new beginning? What might God be doing in your life now? If you were to title this chapter of your life, what would it be? If you were to list your priorities in order, what would they be?

11. Write your story if you can. Assemble a collage if you'd rather. Or dance or sing it. Get it out of your memory and into some expressed form.

When you tell your story, you may not want to give all the details if confidentiality should be maintained. Give the main events, the turning points.

CHAPTER 2

Listening for God (or Discernment)

There is a prophecy in Amos that a time will come when there will be a famine in the land, "Not a famine for bread, nor a thirst for water, but of hearing the words of the Lord." That time has now come to pass. It is the present age.[1]

—R. D. Laing

Blessed Lord, who hast caused all holy Scriptures to be written for our learning; Grant that we may in such wise hear them, read, mark, learn, and inwardly digest them, that by patience and comfort of thy holy Word, we may embrace and ever hold fast the blessed hope of everlasting life, which thou hast given us in our Saviour Jesus Christ. Amen.

—The Book of Common Prayer

When finishing the eight-week Beginning Again course, many people tell me that listening is the most important practice they've discovered. They've learned to better listen to God as the Spirit speaks through their own lives, through other people, through the creation, and through the scriptures.

In our formal education, we are taught to write and to speak. But not much time is given to teaching us to listen. It takes time, practice, and often some guidelines and support.

As some of my older parishioners read the Bible every day, I know they are reading prayerfully—listening to God and the Spirit's word to their hearts. But I see pastor after pastor for whom the Bible is simply a book to read for the purpose of finding sermon material. It doesn't seem to make much difference whether they are charismatic, conservative or liberal, Protestant or Catholic.

Noticing this practice and his students' hunger, Dietrich Bonhoeffer, leader of an underground seminary in Germany during World War II, told his students to meditate on the same small piece of scripture every day for half an hour, and not to drag in commentaries. This was not to be the passage to be preached on for Sunday but simply for their private feeding on the Word of God. His students found it extremely hard.

How can we teach ourselves and our parishioners to read and integrate and really listen to scripture, to what God is saying? Most books are *about* scripture, and not about listening to the living Lord to whom scripture points.

We can learn a lot from an ancient practice of listening and integration developed by monks; it's called *lectio divina* or divine reading. It is a way of being involved with the text, of loving God with one's heart, soul, mind, and strength.

Perhaps it is based on Jesus' teaching in Matthew 7:7:

Ask—and it will be given,
Seek—and you will find,
Knock—and it will be opened unto you.

John of the Cross amplifies this:

Seek in *reading,*
And you will find in *meditation;*
Knock in *prayer,*
And it will be opened to you in *contemplation.*

Lectio was first practiced as a part of corporate prayer; after more traditional prayers, one monk would read a piece of the scripture aloud. There would be silence. The text would be read again. And again. When the listeners had heard it enough, they would go off to their rooms to pray about what they had heard.

In the Middle Ages a monk systematized this in four stages:

Lectio:	Reading, paying attention
Meditatio:	Thinking about the passage, letting it sink in to feeling, to the heart

Oratio: Praying, simply and briefly
Contemplatio: Being with God in the silence

The pattern is not always rigidly sequential, but it is a way to love God, to listen to God, with heart, soul, mind, and strength.

There are some interesting modern variations to this pattern. On a handout at the end of this chapter, I've adapted one "beginner" method written by Canadian Jesuits.

Though we can teach methods for listening and cultivate them in our own lives, hearing and recognizing God's voice ultimately is a spiritual gift, not an achievement that one can master. Methods such as the *lectio* or the Jesuit pattern are like scales on the piano that are helpful for beginners and good reminders for the proficient. They help the mind find receptive patterns. But prayerfulness, begging for the Spirit to teach, is the attitude that makes listening possible.

God is the one who teaches to listen and to pray. We must pray for the gift and pray for the gift to be taught. They say that mature writers have "found their voice." I think we need to "find our ear"— our best way of recognizing God's voice, knowing that, once we have found our ear, God may decide to speak in a different language.

Some people simply cannot listen to God in scripture. Some find God most readily in music or in the outdoors. Contemplation in the Jesuit understanding is paying attention to the reality of God, whether God be in scripture, music, the other person, or in nature. Whenever we get beyond our own small preoccupations, whenever we have some degree of self-transcendence, whenever we are aware of the reality of God, contemplation has begun. If you are absolutely unable to find God in your Bible, go outside, listen to music, do whatever you do that puts you in touch with Something More.

This chapter has focused on listening to God—but active listening to other people also requires hearing with more than the intellect. It is similar to the *lectio* process because it involves hearing with one's imagination and intuition. An active listener reflects to the teller the heart of what is being said.

Many times I've grown as I've listened to what an active listener has said to me about my story. I really took notice when one listener said, "I wonder if you recognize how your face lights up whenever you talk about music?" No, I didn't. Wow! What did that mean for me? He also got me thinking when he said, "Why is it that you've never mentioned your wife in your story?" Oh, no! Sometimes listening means hearing—and reflecting on—what has *not* been said.

Then listening to God also involves listening to ourselves. What is your body saying to you? What are your feelings saying? Your dreams? It's easy to take these communications literally. If I am hungry, it must be for food. But our hungers and desires for friends, for God, for "home," may be disguised in any number of codes that we need to unlock. What is God saying?

John Calvin knew that reason wasn't enough to listen to God. And knowing that only the Holy Spirit can teach us truth, he prayed before and after his lectures:

> May the Lord grant
> That we may contemplate
> The mysteries of His Heavenly wisdom
> With truly increasing devotion,
> To His glory
> And to our edification.

Pray that your heart may seek and may receive. Pray that as you mature, you may be able to listen to scripture and listen to your life and the lives of others—all as books through which God speaks.

Notes for Leaders

• *General helps.* Helping others to listen will be easier if you have already received listening support and direction, if you have been in a group that has helped you practice and be familiar with different patterns of listening.

• *Small-group sessions.* For session 3, I give out and discuss the "Praying with Scripture" handout found at the end of this chapter. You may choose to give out handouts (1) as preparatory homework, or (2) during the session as discussion guides, or (3) at the end of a session as homework to practice what was learned in the session.

If conservatives are afraid of getting away from scripture or objective criteria for discernment, I refer to John Calvin on the subjective and objective ways of knowing: We need the objective criteria of scripture, but only as the Spirit teaches us can we really know. Paul said there was a difference between human wisdom and the personal wisdom that comes from Christ.

In small groups one can turn to many ways to lead meditative prayer that are not acceptable in a Sunday morning worship service. As leader, be sure that *accomplishment* is downplayed: There is no right way to do this, and one doesn't have to participate. Yet inevitably there will be comparisons among members; some will feel their response didn't measure up. Success and failure categories based on comparisons are death to the spiritual life. The focus should be on God and the gift of God.

While some participants will be very verbal and open, others, often men, may find this threatening. I like to present several optional approaches, repeatedly give permission not to "get it," and repeat that we worship the God of experience, not the experience of God. I find that often the limited verbal contribution of the very quiet among us can be profound, and that the talkative ones appreciate the depth.

People do learn to listen better in groups. You might try this: Have people center quietly, and then have a scripture passage read aloud three times. The first time, ask people to respond by repeating a line that stuck with them. The second time, ask them to make a comment about something they heard that caused them to "feel." The third time, ask for responses in the form of brief prayers.

All the elements of the *lectio* are here: scripture, prayer, thinking, feeling, praying, surrounded by silence. Afterwards I invite people to write about their experience and to share those "journal entries" if they care to.

•   *Working with individuals.* The first questions are like those in marriage counseling—to help people listen and speak the truth. A spiritual director helps directees notice inner facts. What did you think? How did that strike you? What happened in you?

The second questions are about the reality of God: How did God react to that? What did God say when you told God how angry you were? We are not trying to arrive at any particular state, but to foster the relationship between God and the individual. This is very hard work; people offer resistance and evasion, clever insights, and personal analysis rather than focusing on an I-Thou (God) relationship.

Helping some beginners, particularly introverted-thinking men, is very difficult. Sometimes God speaks to them what they know is True. Sometimes they say "nothing" happened. Then I ask them about that nothing. Usually "nothing" has a texture or meaning. Sometimes they pass over their own experience because it isn't flamboyant like that of extraverted–feeling women. Intensity is not the issue. Recognizing God's voice is.

• *In congregations.* It's important to start where people are and to try things with a representative small group before springing them on the large group.

Some churches like mine are open to different forms of worship. Others are suspicious of any change. I get a lot of feedback when I ask a few people to join me after the service. They warm up talking about the sermon. I'm always amazed to hear what they heard in relation to what I intended. Then I ask what part of the service meant most to them. If they are open, I'll ask where they experienced God. I am usually delighted and surprised and treasure their insights.

Once group or worship participants have gotten in touch with their experience of God, especially after their experience has been confirmed by others, they have a better touch-point, sensing what inner experiences go along with the word *God.* They can better discern what rings true. They can sort out what ideas, feelings, and intuitions lead to God, which are destructive, and which are neutral. Older evangelicals would call this experience of ringing true "the inner testimony of the Holy Spirit."

• *In the worship service.* The reading and preaching about scripture is adequately covered in most worship services. But most services do not encourage contemplative listening. Maybe the best we can do on ordinary Sundays is to allow time for silence. In my service I allow pauses during the prayer time; this encourages people to do their own praying. I pray before the reading of scripture, that God would speak and that we could really listen. We often leave a pause after the scripture reading. You might leave a brief silence preceding the reading of scripture and after the sermon, to encourage people to reflect, pray, and rest in God.

I find Acts 10—Peter's vision of the sheet with unclean animals—to be a good text for a sermon on listening and discerning God's communication.

• *A model for reading and praying more imaginatively.* The following is a specific model you might use for prayerfully reading Luke 15:11–32.

Find a comfortable place where you can relax, "center," and be open to the Spirit. Breathe deeply. Visualize the light coming in, relaxing your body. (Read the scripture: Luke 15:11–32.)

1. Use your imagination. Put yourself in the story scene as the younger brother . What does he feel? Think like? What is it like to be the elder brother? Get inside him, feel his pain, his anger. What is it like to be the father? Where is the mother?

2. Have a dialogue between the various characters. Let the prodigal in you speak to the father, and the elder brother to the father. What does the father say? You may find it comes easily. You may find that it comes better as you write it down.

3. What if these characters were all within you? Might you dialogue with the angry brother or sister, the scared kid, the loving father, and the host of other characters within? Speak with Jesus about the one with whom you feel the most affinity.

4. Discern. Where is God speaking in this? Don't assume that the Jesus you've been talking with in your imagination is the Lord. Check him out. Does he sound like the Jesus of the New Testament? Is the character of this person giving advice the same as the character of God revealed in scripture? Does the advice lead you closer to God and to your loved ones?

5. Make your response tangible through some ritual. If you are praying for insight, light a candle. If God is trying to smooth off the rough edges of your personality, put a rough pebble in your pocket. Write at least something down in your journal and share it with one trusted person.

Praying with Scripture

God speaks to us. We must be willing to listen.

Listening to God may be like listening to another person at a noisy party. Other people may interrupt. But we hear as we are attentive and relaxed.

Most people hear God best in scripture. (You might not hear God in the Bible if you read it as you read a newspaper.) Others hear better as they listen to creation, music, or their own lives. After a while you will be like the old RCA logo: a dog listening to a phonograph on which he hears "his master's voice." Though there may be surface scratches, God is communicating, loving us.

Prepare yourself to listen. You might focus on your breathing or walk to quiet your spirit.

Ask for the grace to listen. It is a gift, not an accomplishment. You are not setting aside quiet time to pick up ideas about God but to listen to God, to be with God, to be loved, to grow in your relationship with God.

As you listen or sit attentively, something may strike you. You may experience God's love. You may have a new insight. Something wordless may click in your mind. You may feel at home. Something inside may say, *oh yes.* You may feel at home or centered or at peace with a sense of Another.

God is speaking directly through these experiences. What you hear is the inner testimony of the Holy Spirit. Stay there. Don't rush on. Pray about what is happening.

Sometimes "nothing" happens. Pay attention to the nothing. Ask God about it. What does it mean? You may be out of practice and need to wear down your native resistance to God. You may be resisting the obvious things God is saying elsewhere in your life. God may be speaking—to remind you of God's absence.

To pray with scripture try this pattern:

HANDOUT continued

Scripture: Pick a passage and have it handy. You might choose one suggested by someone else (such as daily lectionary readings), choose one reading for a whole week, or be guided daily by the Spirit, depending on your need. Or you might choose a favorite hymn or prayer.

Place: Choose a solitary place where you will be uninhibited in your response to God's presence.

Posture: Relax. Go for a peaceful harmony of body and spirit.

Scripture: Turn to the chosen passage and read it aloud very slowly. Listen to the music of the words. Look at the beauty and allow God to look at you.

Pray: Respond from your heart. Carry on a written or verbal dialogue with God. Allow yourself to be with God.

Adapted from Armand Nigro, S.J., in J. Veltri, S.J., *Orientations* (Guelph, Canada: Loyola House, 1979).

CHAPTER 3

Praying

Prayer is a very natural yet strange activity. A man recovering from alcoholism remembers a night in the hospital. He was delirious, out of his mind. He heard someone yelling out for God. Loudly. Insistently. This agitated him because he didn't believe there was a God. When he returned to his sense, he asked the night nurse who had been crying out to God.

"It was you," she answered.

Praying is so natural that it often goes on without our conscious knowledge. But tragically, with most of us conscious prayer becomes forced or uncomfortable.

I remember trying to pray as a boy. I'd get under the covers (or kneel by the bed when I was serious) and try to say the Lord's Prayer through, thinking about the meaning of every phrase. I'd lose my attention and go back to the beginning.

Where did I get those expectations? From a Roman Catholic baby-sitter? A spiritual director suggests that I wanted to offer God the best that I knew. But with God, the best sometimes gets in the way of the good. Our expectations that God deserves the very best get in the way of our being honest and transparent. Jesus says:

> And when you come before God, don't turn that into a theatrical production either. All these people making a regular show out of their prayers, hoping for stardom! Do you think God sits in a box seat?
>
> Here's what I want you to do: Find a quiet, secluded place so you won't be tempted to role-play before God. Just be there as simply and honestly as you can manage. The focus will shift from you to God, and you will begin to sense his grace (Matt. 6:5–6 TM).

While that is a comforting thought, the idea that we have to offer the best to God often gets in the way of real prayer. Add to that the formal prayers of church that were polite and boring, and it's a tribute to God that we keep on trying.

I remember struggling to write prayers of adoration for the worship service in my first church. Generally I copied prayers from a book. Leading worship, either from the book or from my own writing, didn't help my relationship with God. Just the opposite, it made me feel like the hypocrite I was. My own spiritual life was as empty as it could be, all ideas from others and no connection with my interior life. I read lots of prayer books and nothing helped.

Many who are supposed to be helping the spiritual life of others are similarly bankrupt. After a while, many get used to a wide gulf between professional intellectual abundance and private spiritual scarcity. I see pastors who use set prayers, the "office," or centering prayer. Even though they have the right moves, I am often not impressed with their relationship with God. Likewise, I have seen laypeople who set aside a time for personal prayer but have no real intimacy with God. Then others appear to have a lively relationship. The difference seems to be in their honesty with and willingness to listen to God.

One breakthrough in my ability to be honest with God came during my clinical pastoral training. I got some counseling from my supervisor, the first person who truly listened to me. For the first time in my life, I had said what was really bothering me; I'd said the worst and was accepted. I remember coming home and kneeling and crying. Forgiveness and grace were no longer ideas but parts of my experience. Along with Jacob I felt I had seen God's face and found God's favor.

In continued clinical pastoral training I read the work of Samuel Miller, dean of Harvard Divinity School and writer of classic prayers. Though we were obviously very different people, he expressed my own feelings forthrightly. He wrote a sermon that still inspires me:

> Let your soul speak for itself. Some souls hold conversation with God in music, and some in the sowing of seed, and others in the smell of sawed wood, and still others in the affectionate understanding of their friends. All souls are not alike. Utter your own prayer, in the language of your own joy.
>
> Quit dressing your soul in somebody else's piety. Your soul is not a pauper. Let it live its own life. Untie your soul, give it

room to breathe, let it play, do not be ashamed of it. It is the child
of the eternal and destined for greater things than you dream.[1]

I was facing midlife before prayer became fairly consistently alive
for me, or rather before I became alive in my relationship with God. In
this period I learned lots of languages of prayer, from guided imagery to
the Jesus Prayer to Breath Prayer to Ignatian dialogues or colloquies.
Most helpful was going through an Ignatian thirty-day retreat. Traditionally this is an intensive, virtually silent month-long stretch, but I partici-
pated in an alternative form: The exercises were stretched out over a
year, an hour a day; I met with a director for an hour a week.

An hour a day seemed *so* long. I mightily resisted my own prayerful listening by reading about the exercises and what I was meant to
achieve. But here I was supposed to listen to God in scripture, not for
the purpose of preaching but simply to apply it to my life. I was supposed to notice what God was doing inside me, to pray for specific
graces, and to read the Bible as though it were addressed to me. I was
used to analyzing my feelings and the Bible but not used to listening to
God in the feelings, thoughts, and intuitions roused as I prayed through
the Bible.

Early on I noted my spiritual director's comment that God would
teach me how to pray. I began to get the idea that prayer wasn't a good
work or something to be achieved but a relationship very much like any
other relationship. As the Spirit guided me from within, as I was receptive to that Spirit, our relationship grew stronger.

Paul's words made more and more sense: "Likewise the Spirit
helps us in our weakness; for we do not know how to pray as we ought,
but that very Spirit intercedes with sighs too deep for words" (Rom.
8:26).

Those sighs deeper than words may be called prayerfulness. Words
are usually necessary, but one can be prayerful without words. Being
grateful is being prayerful. Moments that quench the thirst of the heart
are prayerful. God is sighing in us; that is an attitude of prayer, living in
the Spirit, our minds and our hearts knowing the reality of God.

Pay attention! Just as it was for the delirious alcoholic, prayer is
going on beyond or beneath our conscious awareness. Our job is to wake
up, to invite God into our consciousness, into our awareness, into our
wills. God does not invade or come in until we consciously wake up
and say yes. God is always there, standing and knocking at the door of
awareness. We have to open the door.

We struggle against knowing who God really is. That is probably one of the best arguments for the reality of God: Real relationships by nature are iconoclastic. My wife and my friends always surprise me with their otherness; I have to surrender the pictures in my mind to their reality. Likewise, God is always destroying our idols, our images of what God *ought* to be like. If God were just a figment of my mind, a wish-fulfillment, our vital relationship would not have this image-destroying quality.

When I step away from my intellectual approach and listen to music, I can get in touch with the longings of my heart. If I can kneel or cross myself, I'm reminded that my body knows how to pray even when my mind doesn't. When I turn to the Psalms or to other Bible passages through which God has spoken to me before, I am often aware of prayer taking place. But I can't *make* it happen. I *can* pray for the gift of prayer. For true prayer is from God to God through me.

I find it helpful to remember a phrase from Ignatius. It is God asking the question: "What is it you want?" As I listen for God asking me that question, I can get beneath the pious phrases I've traditionally identified with prayer. Usually what I want is not some thing, but a grace, an attitude. Sometimes it is guidance. More and more it is God. Lately my response to God has been: "What I want is you and your love." And when I ask Jesus what he wants from me, I hear, "You and your love."

We need to remember that emotional intensity is not a guarantee of a valid prayer. Goose bumps or tears are not a measure of faith. We can encourage people and model active prayer, but perhaps the best "help" is to remind the child in all of us that we don't have to "get it right." What God wants is us, our hearts. In the words of Dom John Chapman, a wise old Englishman, "The best way to pray is the way you pray best."[2]

Notes for Leaders

•   *In small-group sessions.* For this session on prayer I use the "Meditative Prayer" handout found at the end of this chapter. I encourage participants to pray without words and to receive God's love without words.

I suggest a prayer exercise that Gerald May used in a workshop I attended: Ask people to be quiet and focus for a moment on their breath. Then ask them to be prayerful. Suggest that they all have some kernel of experience identifying the attitude of true prayer. Suggest that they ask God for that gift. Phrases such as *listen to God, let go and let God,* or *open yourself to the Spirit* might help them understand this contemplative prayer. I repeat this theme again and again: Being prayerful is a gift from God, not an achievement of ours. Allow the group to sit in silence, which encourages people to go within and not be distracted. In this exercise most people sense the Spirit praying in them.

Then ask people to write about what happened, what they sensed, felt, thought. Ask if they would read or paraphrase their comments to one other person or to the whole group. Ask for reflective comments from listeners. As facilitator, carefully accept comments, affirming what people have experienced and suggesting how this exercise might be applied to one's daily life.

I make it clear that people don't have to participate in the exercise. I don't introduce this style of prayer with young evangelicals because even when I use scripture, they tend to identify it as being too "New Age." It is a matter of being familiar with your group (and they with you) and judging where the group is.

• *In the parish.* I make sure that a number of people lead prayers and prayer exercises. Hearing other people pray aloud is "permission giving." In public my lay leaders tend to give more transparent prayers than I do, and this helps break down people's resistance to being honest with God.

Almost all of my lay leaders have identified a prayer form that is most natural to them. Some use music; others introduce silence. We model several sorts of prayer so as not to suggest that there is one "best" way to pray.

• *In worship services.* Generally I sense that people are more open to experiments in the small-group setting than in the Sunday morning worship service. In the larger context, I suggest that any changes be gradual. Silence needs to be introduced slowly, with instructions for using it.

With the whole congregation I lead "bidding" prayers. At the beginning of the "pastoral" prayer, I usually ask for the gift of the Spirit and encourage people to breathe deeply, visualize the light of God, or just be still and know that God is God. Then I "bid" people to give prayers of thanksgiving, for others, for themselves. People, especially young and old men, initially resisted this. But now they often say that it has encouraged them to do their own praying.

The "Meditative Prayer" handout may be a model for introducing this form of prayer in a worship service. Explain what you propose beforehand, possibly in the bulletin, and give people permission not to participate. Then lead the prayer as presented at the end of this chapter.

• Recently I've realized how much people want "tradition," the same thing, every Easter and Christmas Eve. We may want to try to do something new, but even the young and adventuresome want the old stories in the old language and in the old style. It's like reading to the children at night when you tell an old story; they want the old words. That's part of the ritual that makes it powerful. When I go to a Jewish Bar Mitzvah, I am overwhelmed with how old this ceremony is. Sometimes I introduce new things by saying that they are very old, which is true. Breath prayer, the Jesus Prayer, meditation and contemplation—it's all there in the Bible. It is we who have become narrow and rationalistic.

A young mother tells me that when she introduces new family rituals, she is generally resisted. But usually the second year she is surprised to see some anticipation of the "new" rituals.

If you're introducing new prayer patterns into church services, expect resistance. Keep in touch with what has been, how people have found God before. And believe that the Holy Spirit will teach you to pray, will pray in you with sighs too deep for words.

Meditative Prayer

We breathe out all that separates us from you, O God. We
breathe out even as Jesus did, saying, "Abba, into thy hands I
commit my spirit." We commit, we surrender ourselves to you,
breathing out all that separates us, our doubts, fears, worries
about tomorrow, regrets about the past.

And we breathe in your Holy Spirit, seeing the light come in
and filling our chests and abdomens. Jesus, as you breathed on
the disciples, saying, "Receive the Holy Spirit," may we receive
your Spirit.

When we are distracted, may we have grace to return our
attention to our breath—to you—and let you center us.

PAUSE.

We remember this past week, the gifts that we received. We
remember them with thanks.

PAUSE.

We lift up our loved ones into your light. We picture them one
by one in the light . . . in your arms.

PAUSE.

We tell you our hearts' desires, what we long for. Help us
receive you and your intention.

PAUSE.

We listen to your word, your love for us.

PAUSE.

O God, who has taught us that in returning and rest we shall

HANDOUT continued

be saved, in quietness and confidence shall be our strength—lift
us, we pray, into your presence, where we may be still and know
that you are God, through Jesus Christ our Lord. Amen.

CHAPTER 4

Your Practice

You're hungry? If I asked you what you generally did to meet that need, you wouldn't feel awkward or embarrassed, would you?

You're spiritually hungry? If you dared to admit the need, you might well be embarrassed if I asked how you got fed. Why are people uncomfortable talking about their spiritual practice— how they listen to God, pray, and discern God's activity? This can be as scary to talk about as sex or death. Yet it is liberating to tell someone how and where we experience God.

Prayer *is* one of the most intimate ways to express our love to God. Jesus said not to cast our pearls before swine, and some people are not to be trusted with our inner life.

Some have been made to feel guilty for not doing their spirituality practices "right." A friend who grew up in an evangelical church was in agony for years, wondering if she had really given herself to Christ. Yes, her "decision" was marked down in her Bible. She had gone through the motions. She had felt feelings. But had she really been converted? Some hear they should read the Bible and pray every day; they try for a while but give up. If their desire to read the Bible has become law or a rigid expectation, they experience a sense of failure—and feel guilty.

In his book *The Awakened Heart,* Gerald May talks about willful resolutions. Too often we judge ourselves in relation to our performance.

> Resolutions mean will power, willpower means achievement, achievement means success and failure, and the whole sequence means losing an appreciation of the gift [of grace].
> Substitute prayer for resolution, hope for expectation, fidelity

for compulsion. Seek to encourage yourself instead of manipulating yourself.

Live, love, and yearn with unbearable passion, but don't try to make it happen and don't try to hold on when it does happen.1

Some years ago, when I thought I wanted to be a therapist, I was part of the Church of the Saviour in Washington, D.C. At the time I was greatly offended by their continual discussions about personal spiritual disciplines. I thought the group was preoccupied with spiritual one- up-manship. But later, when I faced my midlife crisis and wanted to grow spiritually, I turned to these folks, knowing how seriously they took their inner journeys. At that time I stumbled on these marvelous words about spiritual disciplines, written by Elizabeth O'Connor, a member of that church.

What often happens is that disciplines are pressed on those who may not be on any journey at all and are quite content where they are. In this way what helps some to be born into freedom becomes the means for delivering others into slavery.2

If the reason for the disciplines is lost and cannot be recovered, throw them out as useless. We should hesitate, however, to discard a discipline on the basis of the resistance or rebellion of one of our many selves, for if it does its work it will raise protest in us and point out the place of our withholding.

Cling to them when they show you what you must overcome to reach what is high in yourself.3

How do we know what practice will meet our spiritual needs? In most religions, the prescription is given. Moslems, for instance, pray five times a day. Jews pray three times daily.

For Christians, thousands of books have been written about patterns of prayer, suggesting one method or another. But the Bible gives no hard and fast rules, though it makes one thing clear: One is encouraged to keep at it. "And Jesus told them a parable about their need to pray always and not to lose heart" (Luke 18:1).

Time, place, duration, and type of prayer or devotional activity vary from person to person. Many extraverts who can't connect with quiet prayer find themselves close to God when they walk and pray out loud. I know some people who pray while running. Others read prayers or pray in groups of two or three.

When it comes to setting up a devotional discipline, we should be gentle with ourselves. Camus, a French spiritual director and friend of Francis de Sales (not to be confused with Albert Camus), gives this discerning advice:

> Be patient with everyone, but especially with yourself. I mean, do not be disheartened by your imperfections, but always rise up with fresh courage. I am glad you make a fresh beginning daily; there is no better means of attaining to the spiritual life than by continually beginning again....The ones who are fretted by their own failings will not correct them; all profitable correction comes from a calm, peaceful mind.4

What patterns are best for me at this point in my life? To answer this I've prioritized my life goals. At the top of the list I've ranked: time with God, time with others, and exercises to improve the quality of my love. What are your priorities? Once I was aware of these longings—my wanting to love and be loved—my daily activities could be seen in a different light. Some were just time killers, space fillers.

Once I'd identified and prioritized my spiritual goals, my spiritual program came from inside me; it was not imposed from without. It didn't come from the parental me ("I ought to") as much as from my true heart (the Spirit's prompting; "I want to").

Once we've prioritized goals, I suggest taking a weekly or monthly personal inventory, to take stock of how we're doing. Are we spending our energy as we really want to? *Inventory* is a business term; it refers to checking one's assets and liabilities. The term is central to the Alcoholics Anonymous program, maybe because the founder was a businessman. The inventory in the twelve steps of AA focuses on one's awareness of poor choices, destructive behavior that may lead to addiction. This type of inventory cuts through denial.

But the inventory I'm suggesting should also look at one's assets, especially one's connection with God and others. Pausing for an "awareness inventory"—of blessings, connection, a sense of belonging—can usher us into heartfelt prayer.

If a relationship with God is among your top priorities, I suggest you consider practicing three patterns of connection: prayer, meditation (or

listening), and inventory. Presented in a different order, these three patterns are AA maintenance steps. Step 10 deals with inventory: "Continued to take personal inventory, and when we were wrong, promptly ad-
mitted it." Step 11 says, "Sought through prayer and meditation to improve our conscious contact with God as we understood him, praying
only for knowledge of his will for us and the power to carry that out."
(Reprinted with permission, Alcoholics Anonymous World Services Inc.)

A friend, for many years in AA, explained how this worked in
practical terms: "First, I think over the day and thank God for the good
stuff. Then I think if there was any bad stuff. If it's my fault, I make
amends first thing in the morning if I can. If I'm sore about the way
someone else treated me, I take it up with them right away. Then I pray
for my family and the people I work with and lie down and sleep."

The Jesuits call this practice "examination of conscience" (or consciousness). Their founder, Ignatius of Loyola, recommended that his
followers practice the examination twice a day, for fifteen minutes each
time. He purportedly said that if his followers couldn't read the Bible or
say their prayers on a particular day, they should at least do the examination of conscience because this kept them in touch with what God was
doing in their lives.

Most of us can benefit from a structure to keep us pointed in the
right direction. Too often we live under the tyranny of the urgent, for-
getting what is truly important. This point is made well by Stephen
Covey in *The Seven Habits of Highly Effective People.*[5] He tells the
story of a man cutting wood with a saw. At first he was making great
headway, working efficiently, really stacking up the wood. But a week
later a friend stopped by and noticed the woodcutter was working harder
but with less to show for it. "What's the matter?" asked the friend.

"Oh, the saw is dull."
"Why don't you sharpen it?"
"I don't have time. I'm too busy."

In Covey's scheme effective people are not driven by the tyranny of
the urgent. We can't afford to work with dull saws. "Sharpen the saw,"
he says. That means we need to take care of ourselves physically, emotionally, socially, and spiritually. He takes a weekly personal inventory,
checking his week against his life goals.

I have taken up this habit, but I find I need help; I share my inventory with several support groups. Some organized and motivated people do well without a group. But most of us, particularly clergy and church leaders, need to be reminded of what is really important. I regularly ask my governing board how they are doing, or rather, what God is doing in their lives. This helps us maintain a sense of openness to each other and to God.

And as we are open to God, we can become truly effective, increasingly finding our "center" in our hearts—in God's presence or word inside us—not in our work and accomplishments.

Notes for Leaders

• *In small-group sessions.* In this session I use two handouts, found at the end of this chapter: (1) "Criteria for Discernment" (for mature Christians) and (2) "Five Minutes with God." This second handout I also use with parishioners and people who are beginning spiritual direction. It is modified from AA twelve steps, from Bill Hybels's book *Too Busy Not to Pray,* and from the Ignatian examination of conscience. I give this form differing titles, depending on my audience. With people familiar with twelve steps, I call it "Inventory." With Roman Catholics, I call it "Examen." With my parishioners and evangelicals, I call it "Five Minutes with God."

I suggest that the inventory or examen include some writing. When it comes to writing, people usually resist. I urge people to write just a little each day, a reflection on the day and a brief thank you to God for the gifts. Some people go overboard and write volumes. (Few keep it up over the long term.) Some do a once-over-lightly during the week and spend an hour or so on Sunday adding "flesh" to the bare bones. Some people write little when they seem centered, but go at it earnestly when they face transitions, feel pain, or are not aware of God's presence.

Most people give up many times. It might be sheer laziness. Maybe God really isn't a high priority. Sometimes they don't want to see their sins in God's light. Any intentional practice is almost inevitably accompanied by resistance.

• The following five steps and questions help people identify and prioritize goals or values. Once these are clarified, spiritual practice can be motivated from within.

1. List the priorities in your life. Rank them in order.
2. What do you do to help keep yourself focused on your priorities?
3. Take steps to write down these priorities and share your commit ments with another person.
4. What, if any, regular practice do you try to maintain to help you feed your spiritual hunger?
5. Where is the growing edge in you, a desire for more contact with God and others that a new or expanded practice might support?

- The following is a "very short examen" reminder.

Stop:	Breathe deeply, breathing in Spirit.
Look:	At your day: name one delight, one sorrow.
Listen:	To your life. What question does it ask?
Pray:	From your life, from your heart.
Listen:	To God. What does God say?

Let go and know that I am God.

- *In the larger congregation.* We take regular corporate inventories with our leadership group. With the congregation we try to take an annual inventory. One way to carry out these inventories is to look at our congregation's mission statement and against that we measure where our energy, money, and time is going. Another way is to measure the evidence of the fruit of the Spirit, listed in Galatians 5. The inventory is about marking relationships, not our numbers or our good works.

Criteria for Discernment

1.   Does it sound like God? We recognize God's voice when it reverberates in resonance with scripture, with the history of tradition and reason, with the advice of mature Christians, and with our own deepest knowledge of God's activity in our lives.

2.   Does it fit me uniquely? Does this leading fit my gifts, my personality? Am I responding not so much to an "ought" but to an inner sense of certainty?

3.   Is Jesus Lord? Does this lead to my getting puffed up or debased, making this my project, or is it God's glory I seek? If it has to go my way, perhaps I have been caught by something other than the Holy Spirit.

4.   What are the fruits? Are the results found in numbers or in character and spirituality? Is the fruit of the Spirit evident? Is there inner compulsion or freedom? Do I have time for God, for others, for myself?

Five Minutes with God

One half minute: *prepare.* Quiet yourself, sing a hymn, prepare your body, mind, spirit. Ask for the gift of the Spirit.

One minute: *yesterday.* Look over the day, particularly what was happening inside yourself. What are you grateful for? What are you sorry about? What is God trying to teach you?

One minute: *prayer.* How do you respond to all that? What is your deepest longing beside thanks and confession and concern for others?

One minute: *listen.* To God's response. God may answer your prayer, or confirm what you have noticed. God may have a different agenda.

One minute: *plan.* What will be your priorities today, this week, after you have received some nudging or calling?

One–half minute: *rest.* Just be with God. Enjoy.

1.   This "five minutes" may be expanded or contracted. If you are really rushed, at least look over your day and say a quick prayer. "Help" and "thanks" are very basic.

2.   You might "prepare" by *prayerfully* running, walking, or glancing heavenward. You might sing or read scripture. Your setting is not important; the direction you look at is. Look to God.

3.   For extraverts, looking at yesterday probably starts with actions outside yourself. But move toward the inner thoughts, feelings, movements of the Spirit. What is going on in external history and inner reality? This may include dreams, slips, a subtle awareness of God. Consider a brief scripture reading. If you do nothing more than thank God, that is enough.

4.   Your prayer may be set, memorized, coordinated with your breath, or blurted out as to a friend. You may write it, dance it,

sing it. What do you really want? What is the Spirit already praying in you?

5.   Listen. This may be difficult at first. Many people think this
through: "I'm sick with a cold; my body and perhaps God are telling me to slow down." Some people reflect on the movements of
their feelings, sorting out God's call from other voices. It may be
helpful to ask, "What is God calling me to change or be? Where is
God calling me to go?" I often ask, "What are you telling me?"
Often I receive an immediate response, such as: "Cut out that
self-pity." Go with the answer if it sounds like God. Check it out
with a group or a wise friend. Check it out with the character of
God as revealed in tradition and scripture. You may hear the
word addressed to you in the shower or out walking. Your enemy
or spouse may confront you. God whispers to us in our dreams,
speaks to us in scripture, and shouts to us in our pain.

6.   Plan. Do you spend quality time taking care of yourself?
What is your plan for the day, week, month? Do first things first,
from the inside out, listening to God.

7.   Be with God. Enjoy your company, God's company.

8.   Write the results in a journal at least weekly. Also, weekly,
ask yourself, "Am I on course— living according to my priorities,
God's wish?" Discuss your journey with a group or a friend. This
makes your journey more tangible and links you with others.
Ideally, write at least a sentence every day; ask for what you want
and listen to God. Try it and talk over how it goes with someone
you trust. That's the beginning of spiritual direction.

CHAPTER 5

Our Personality Patterns

*We shall find when we look into our own souls or those with whom
we have to deal that there is an immense variation among them,
both in aptitude and in method of approaching God.[1]*

*A respect for every type and size, homey patience.... These are the
qualities which make a good director. Even with the young and
untried, routine instructions and methods are often dangerous; for
already, at the beginning, soul differs immensely from soul.[2]*

—Evelyn Underhill

I well remember the first person who came to me for advice about her
spiritual life. She was out of touch with God and wanted some help. I
told her and gave her material explaining what worked for me. She was
grateful, but she came back and said that none of it worked.

Newly familiar with the Myers–Briggs Type Indicator (MBTI), I
gave a version of it to her and found that she was temperamentally different from me in every category. About this same time I attended a
Roman Catholic conference on MBTI and spirituality. In a small–group
session, I met a nun who had the exact psychological profile as my parishioner. At my request the nun wrote down prayer patterns that worked
for her. I thought her version reflected a strange Roman Catholic piety,
yet I gave it to my parishioner. She was effusive! Yes, it worked.

Then and there I became converted to using the MBTI to help people
discover hints to the spiritual practices—kinds of prayer, meditation, and
inventory—that best suit them temperamentally.

The MBTI measures the personality patterns identified by Swiss psychiatrist Carl Jung. The MBTI, one of the standard battery of tests used by psychologists around the world, is not really an objective test, because it reflects our knowledge of ourselves. It does not measure sickness. It helps us discern our gifts. It has been widely used for management, teaching, and spiritual development. It encourages self–acceptance and self–knowledge, and I believe that self-knowledge and self–acceptance are the beginning stages of spiritual-psychological growth. It is a way of teaching people to work with people of different temperaments.

A psychologist friend of mine was asked to consult with a Trappist monastery. Two of the monks were always in trouble, and the abbot thought there might be some pathology or at least some dysfunctional family–system issues. My friend gave tests and listened to the monks and found nothing. He decided at last to give the MBTI, and there was the clue! Sure enough, all the monks were high introverts with the exception of the two "offenders." They were extraverts. They moved these two men to jobs where they would see the public, and the introverts settled happily back into the silence!

For spiritual growth, the MBTI helps describe the psyche, the container for—not the content of—our spiritual life.

Most books and teachers about the spiritual life do not acknowledge differences in temperaments. The MBTI helps us cherish differences and helps provide some hints about the shape of our spiritual growth. Here are some hints for beginners.

Extravert or Introvert?

In Jung's theory, the most commonly understood choice we make is being an extravert or an introvert. This choice involves how we look at the world. Extraverts focus their attention toward the outside and get energy by doing so. Introverts look inward.

Naturally, this affects the way we pray. Extraverts usually say they pray better with their eyes open, often out of doors or maybe in front of a picture or listening to music. They don't naturally take to having a "quiet time." They need to push themselves to be quiet and to check out what God has been doing inside. In a group, extraverts will speak first and think "on their feet." Introverts, on the other hand, find it easy to be still but hard to share with others the fruits of their reflection. In a group they may need to be encouraged to speak, but by the time they do they have thought through their comments.

Many who write about prayer—or enter monasteries—are introverts. This may make extraverts feel guilty and see themselves as second–class spiritual seekers.

God certainly created extraverts and introverts, and both have a lot to offer the other. We aren't meant to follow someone else's path; we are meant to start where we are. In groups, both types need to be validated.

Sensing or Intuitive?

Jung suggests that there are two major ways of perceiving the world: by sensing or by intuition. Sensing types pick up information, facts, and concrete items of the world in specific chunks. These people see the trees. The intuitives see the forest, the patterns, the big picture.

Sensing types see the details in scripture. They often can't jump to the abstract principles and various levels of meaning. Young sensing types can sound like the Samaritan woman at the well, whose story is found in John 4. She sees that Jesus is thirsty. But when Jesus talks about living water, she doesn't get it. Conversely, these sensing types may see details in their meditations that intuitives are rarely aware of.

Intuitives jump to the inner meaning of things but may jump right over the facts. They may have trouble with numbers, time, details that are important to sensing types. Intuitives will pick up nuances from spiritual reading but may need to write down what they feel God is call-ing them to do. In groups they may go off on tangents that potentially irritate the sensates.

When I was a boy, my mother and father would discuss the Sunday service at dinner. My father would like the orthodox, solid parts of the sermon. Mother would pick up on the poetry and the mystical sections. It was as though they had been to different churches. I now see that they saw the world through two lenses, Father being a sensing type and Mother being intuitive. Both types can learn to value the gifts of the other.

Thinking or Feeling?

Jung identifies another set of differences—in the way we make decisions. Thinkers rely on logic, weighing the probabilities, the pros and cons. Feelers rely on values and meaning. Thinkers want to know what is true; feelers, what is good. As a group, thinkers are not more intellectual than feelers; rather, feelers are generally more in touch with their feelings than thinkers.

In prayer, feelers want their hearts to be warmed; they need to balance this predisposition with their thinking faculties. Thinking types may be outnumbered in church and may pray from principles; they may need to learn to trust their hearts.

Judging or Perceiving?

A fourth pair of preferences helps distinguish whether a person lives predominantly in a judging (conclusion–drawing) realm or in the perceiving (sensing or intuitive, information-gathering) realm.

Judging types like to draw conclusions, often before all the facts are in. Their time for prayer often has a definite order; they may resist any changes in the order of service or the liturgy. It may be hard for God to break into the routine. They need to pray for the gift of spontaneity.

Perceivers prefer to get more and more information before making a decision. It may be hard for them to set aside a definite time for prayer and to stick to a disciplined routine. They need to pray for the gift of order.

Notes for Leaders

•   *In congregations.* To introduce the MBTI to a congregation, one pastor preached a series of sermons on biblical characters, each one illustrating a different temperament. My approach this year was to preach a sermon about how God makes us unique, and how we need help in learning how God made others. Then I invited people to stay to a short half–hour introduction to the MBTI. I passed out hints for different sorts of prayer for each temperament. That was enough to get most of the motivated people on board, particularly as we followed up in small groups and helped people find specific types of prayer. In my presentations I rely heavily on anecdotal material, describing people of various temperaments.

A minimum instruction usually takes an hour or ninety minutes. I prefer having people take the MBTI as part of a testing program given by a qualified user of the MBTI, who can avoid dangers of misinterpretation. This way, when I follow up with the spiritual development material, I don't have to worry about helping people identify the four letters that reflect their personality; they already know their type.

When I don't have this luxury, when I am dealing with a group that has some psychological sophistication or will not be using the material in an area where it can do much damage, I give the short sorter, "Finding a Fit," found at the end of this chapter, and ask them to work through it quickly. There will always be some people on the boundaries between categories. This usually reflects some changes going on in their lives. Many experts believe that there is a life–long "true type." Some people can't figure out which pattern is theirs even after they take the computer–scored test. But if you explain that sometimes it is difficult to determine one's pattern and continue to work with the group, most people will sort it out over time.

See the bibliography for more information about MBTI types. For starters, it is helpful simply to help people see the value in all types. Explain that this material gives only *hints;* people can use any kind of spiritual practice they find helpful, and God calls people of any temperament to particular jobs that need to be done.

People who are unsophisticated about tests may give too much credence to material like this. In such cases the "hint" factor needs to be stressed even more.

And skeptical people may have trouble believing there is any help to be found in these patterns. You might suggest they take a stab at answering the questions (below). Suggest that this is like trying on clothes—to see if they fit. Usually intuitive–thinkers are very skeptical of the whole thing, and need to study the written material for a long time. Intuitive–feelers can find it quite exciting and "overdo."

• *Small groups or with individual people.* In this session I use the "Finding a Fit" handout, at the end of this chapter. You might give this out at the end of the previous session on "practice," and ask them to answer the questions as homework. Or have participants answer as part of the group session.

The "Finding a Fit" questionnaire is not the MBTI; a trained professional needs to administer the indicator. But this inventory will likely help people get a better glimpse of a personal style of spirituality.

After people have determined their type (four letters), I walk through an explanation of the types (main text of this chapter). I then use the "Reflection Questions" handout to promote reflection, discussion, and writing.

How does what we've learned about ourselves give us hints about our prayer practice and daily examen? In an intentional prayer time, high Ps will need some structure, but a lot of freedom within the structure. High Js will need to let go a little of their need for structure, and pay attention to what God is doing rather than holding on to their structure. In either case, people who are rigidly structured during the day may need a less structured time with God. People who come to God through one function may find that God comes to them through its opposite. (I approach God through intellect, but God reveals love to me through my feeling.)

A third handout "Identifying a Temperament" further introduces the MBTI. This helps people identify themselves in one of four temperament types. It is helpful for participants to have worked through this handout before the material in chapter 6, "Surrender and Control." It might be completed in the group session or done as homework after this session.

• *In spirituality groups.* If there are enough people, I lead the following exercise: I divide the large group into four subgroups, by temperament. I ask each group to prepare a worship service for another temperament group. I assign a coordinator to report back on the group's finished project. I ask another person in each group to report about the process of how the group went about its work. I tell them this is like an open book exam and give them the descriptions of temperaments presented in the chapter, above.

SJs, probably 60 percent of the congregation, will want tradition and appreciate the service being what it has always been. They appreciate calls to duty and want the organizational structure to be clear and effective.

NTs, a minority except in college communities, like intellectual clarity. They usually respond best to more classical music, or at least "classy music" and words that reflect God's glory and majesty. They want clarity and coherence in preaching.

NFs will like the language of spirituality and becoming, and like stories of possibilities and longing. NFPs will want variety all the time, or at least minor changes or informality in the service each week.

SPs, usually grossly underrepresented, will like action songs, gospel or folk music that involves their whole being. They are great at responding to crisis and to sermons that promote that way of thinking.

The exercise is always instructive and usually lots of fun. They have to study their notes to see how another temperament ticks. It's like asking French speakers to get inside a German mentality. It's interesting to see how well they do. Sometimes they overdo with a broad brush. I ask the group for which the service was prepared to give some instant feedback. Then I ask the process reporters to give their feedback. Even if people think the MBTI is nonsense, this usually makes them believers. The four temperament types are radically different in the way they go about their work.

SJs proceed orderly, and get their instructions clear.

SPs get right into activity with little regard for instructions or structure.

NTs usually delight in the design and may have to be dragged away from the assignment because they are arguing over possibilities.

NFs may not get to the work right away, but spend time getting to know each other. They may have rather grandiose plans but miss the facts.

In doing this exercise everyone sees and hears for themselves how these differences work out in planning and in worship.

• *Congregational committees.* I try to get representatives of the four temperaments on the worship committee.

Each congregation has a unique personality, partially due to its history, its social climate, its former pastors, and the combination of personalities intersecting with the grace of God. It is possible to say that the congregation has an MBTI profile. A new book by Bridges (see bibliography) helps each organization discover its profile. The same thing is true with a congregation as with an individual: We need to start where people are and then see where God is leading. To complement a pastor's strengths, the nominating committee might put people of different temperaments around the pastor. With the help of the MBTI, the congregation will be able to celebrate differences as God-given.

• *Spiritual direction.* Knowledge of the four temperaments (not all sixteen types) is adequate for those providing congregational leadership, and it is usually enough for group leaders. But spiritual directors should know how all sixteen combinations suggest patterns for beginning, mid-life, and for mature spiritual seekers. I have written a booklet that offers this information (see the bibliography).

Finding a Fit

Using a "vacation" frame of mind (answering the way you *like* to be rather than the way you *have* to be at work or at home), choose the description in each of the following four pairs that fits you best. Pick the one that seems easiest. Assume that you are capable of exhibiting the qualities in both columns, and you may have to develop particular qualities, especially at work. But, like left– or right–handedness, for most people one is easier, takes less energy, is dominant.

If you have trouble choosing, remember yourself as a teenager. Or remind yourself that you're "on vacation." If that doesn't help, take a second look at the right column. The traits in the left column are encouraged by our culture. This shapes all of us, and those who naturally belong in the right column may have a hard time choosing between their natural inclinations and the qualities that have been necessary for survival.

Extraversion (E)

I . . .

Am energized by the external world
Like to share work
Talk to think and process
Need many relationships
Learn by doing
Am usually friendly, talkative
Scan the environment

Introversion (I)

I . . .

Am energized by the inner world
Work alone contentedly
Think, then talk and act
Need a few good friends
Understand before doing
Am usually reserved at first
Scan inwardly

Which best expresses the way you like to be most of the time, E or I?

_____

Sensing (S)

I . . .

Am careful about the facts
Like the observable and definite
Learn best by examples
Live in the present
Like to apply what I've learned
Prefer to use developed skills
Like to start at the beginning,
go in order

Intuition (N)

I . . .

May make errors of fact
Like to irn by seeing the big picture
Live in the future
Like concepts
Prefer learning new skills
Jump in anywhere, may skip steps

Which best expresses the way you like to be most of the time, S or N?

_____

Thinking (T)

I . . .

Am good at analyzing ideas
Spontaneously find flaws
Use logic to make decisions
Need to achieve
Need to be treated fairly
May enjoy arguments

Feeling (F)

I . . .

Am good at making others feel
good
Spontaneously praise
Use values to make decisions
Need to be appreciated
Need approval
Avoid confrontation and anger

Which best expresses the way you like to be most of the time, T or F?

_____

Judging (J)	Perceiving (P)
I . . .	I . . .
Live by schedules	Live spontaneously
Need structure	Need variety
Plan work, work the plan	Adapt freely
Am decisive, want closure	Am curious, want openness
Take on what can be done	May overschedule
Prepare for the worst	Find it hard to prepare

Which best expresses the way you like to be most of the time, J or P?
_____

What are your four letters? _____

Reflection Questions

1. Note again your four letters.

2. How do the first preferences (E or I) affect the way you relate to others and to God?

3. How do the second preferences (S or N) affect the way you sense or intuit the presence of God?

4. How do the third preferences (T or F) help you recognize your patterns for making decisions? What do you need help with?

5. What insight do you get from the fourth preferences (J or P) about discipline or spontaneity in your life? What do you need help with?

Identifying Your Temperament

The simplest way to remember and apply the MBTI to one's spiritual growth is to try to identify oneself in a specific temperament. Ancient Greeks, Native Americans, and classical students of personality have recognized four basic temperaments. Using the four MBTI pairs we could identify sixteen types, but for now let's just try on for size the four categories.

Note again your four letters:

If your second letter was N, what was your third letter?

If your second letter was S, what was your fourth letter?

Look at the column below that corresponds to your second and third **or** fourth letters. Do you see hints of your natural temperament?

	NF	NT	SJ	SP
NEED	authenticity	competence	sense of belonging	freedom
FOCUS ON	relationships	knowledge	utility	competition
SPIRIT ORIENTING	mystic	theology	duty	celebration
IN GROUP	praise	plan	caution	lead
LEARNS BEST BY	learner-centered groups	content-centered groups	teacher-centered groups	project-centered groups
STRESSOR	insincerity	powerlessness	insubordination	constraint
REWARDED BY	nurturing	confirmation of competence	appreciation	shared experience
SEEKS	new quests	new projects	community	change
PRAYER	loving relationship	awe and mystery	duty	delight
MEDITATES	loving thoughts	reverent thoughts	traditional thoughts	thinking while doing
AS I TAKE SPIRITUAL IINVENTORY I	find it hard to focus on specifics	focus on content and ideas	focus on structured details	see details
FAVORITE GOSPEL	Luke	John	Matthew	Mark
HERO	Luther	Calvin	Ignatius	Francis
HEROINE	Mary, sister of Martha	Evelyn Underhill	Martha	Mother Teresa

(continued)

	NF	NT	SJ	SP
SPIRITUAL FORMATION GROUPS	prayer groups open to the Spirit	study groups open to new truth	traditional group that shares ritual	setting where I notice God as I go with the flow
SEES GOD AS	beauty, heart	truth, justice	unity, duty	action, doing

My favorite Gospel is _____ .
A hero might be _____ .
A heroine might be _____ .
I might be most comfortable in a _____ .
I see God as _____ .

(The preceding chart is adapted from Louise C. Giovannoni, Linda V. Berens, Sue A. Cooper, Introduction to Temperament, *10–11. Published by Telos Publications, 16152 Beach Blvd., Suite 117, Huntington Beach, CA 92649.)*

HANDOUT continued

1. What do you see that is helpful for you? What is "right on"?

2. Does the chart accurately identify your learning style? Your type of prayer?

3. Consider any hints for how you could encourage spiritual growth (see "I feel rewarded by," "I seek out," "I might be most comfortable in").

4. If you were a small–group leader and teaching a new way of prayer, how might you speak the language of each temperament––NF, NT, SJ, SP?

5. If you were preaching about prayer, how might you touch the hearts and minds of each temperament—NF, NT, SJ, SP?

CHAPTER 6

Surrender and Control

The course of life teaches some people hard lessons about surrender. This might be true of a mother who has let go of children. Or recovering alcoholics. Or someone who has retired from a demanding career. Surrender rarely comes easily. And what we most need to surrender to God can depend upon our temperament.

What is the center–point of a particular personality? It might be "what others think" or an addiction or freedom—or any internalized value.

The movie *The Remains of the Day* is a vivid picture of a butler whose center is *duty*. In his novel *The Great Divorce,* C. S. Lewis imagines the inhabitants of hell being offered a joy ride to heaven, where they can stay if they will surrender their besetting sin. Examples? Self–pity; controlling mother–love for a child; even a preacher's love for his profession. Character after character must decide to break free from a besetting sin or return to hell. The choices are wrenching. Whose will will be done? C. S. Lewis said there were essentially only two kinds of people: those who say "God's will be done" and those to whom God will ultimately say "your will be done."

Each of us has a personal pattern for self–centeredness, and the Myers–Briggs Temperament Indicator (MBTI) may help us recognize our own patterns.

Each temperament represents an ego's pattern for organizing reality. Without surrender to God, each temperament is organized around a false self, an idol—sickness or addiction or immaturity . . . anything but the living God. We'll call this a temperament's besetting "compulsive self–image." The false self can be understood as a need to control, to act like God. In a more healthy state, that same temperament shines with a "graceful self–image." Many of us alternate between the two, reverting to the compulsive self–image when we are Hungry, Angry, Lonely, or Tired. (You might remember these with the acronym HALT.)

Each of the four temperaments may have an image of God based on its need to control. We'll call this a temperament's "controlling image of God." But when given over to God, that same temperament thrives with a "graceful image of God."

Unless we choose and choose again to center our lives in principles or values greater than our egos, at times of stress and doubt, we will fall back on these immature and destructive images of a destructive self and a false god. Our lives will be built on sinking sand rather than solid rock.

In a twelve–step meeting a newly recovering woman said she didn't believe in God or a higher power. "That's fine," said her sponsor. "Can you at least believe that *you* aren't God?" That first step of releasing control can be a major shift of consciousness.

Let's look at each of the four temperaments and how it typically exemplifies its false self, its need to control:

Sensing–judging types (SJs) are hard working, reliable, and trustworthy. They hear the call to responsibility and duty and are prepared to face "the worst." They are the authors of job descriptions and do well in structured organizations; in most churches they are the trustees, the administrators and teachers.

Their weaknesses include an inability to see and admit their own limits or focus on their own needs. They are rarely interested in self–discovery and shy away from self–disclosure. They often see themselves as being simple and uncomplicated, the guardians of tradition, the salt of the earth.

They are prime candidates for addiction, burnout, and codependence. They may feel responsible for everyone in the organization and become angry when others don't do their part.

The biblical Martha was most likely a compulsive SJ. When they are in their destructive mode, God seems like an unfair judge, always laying more laws and guilt on them. Like the prodigal's older brother, they may be angry at God, angry at others, and unable to come to the table of celebration. They may wind up out in the cold.

Ignatius of Loyola was an SFJ. He tried storming heaven by being excessively spiritual but finally surrendered this to God. As he found God in all things, he taught others to notice the God of grace through a daily examination of consciousness.

For SJs surrender involves facing their limits, their humanity, their "not being God." Their basic sin is idolatry, making an idol of their sense of responsibility. Surrender involves living by grace rather than law, giving freely and not under compulsion. In community this may mean encouraging others to do their part. Surrender also means seeing God not as the law giver as much as the love giver.

Sensing–perceiving types (SPs) know how to enjoy life and can fully live in the present, while looking forward to more enjoyment. Whereas SJs deny themselves for future enjoyment, SPs have difficulty denying themselves at all. In Aesop's fable, they are the grasshoppers, the SJs are the ants. As you might imagine, SPs feel judged by the SJs of the world.

Some of this is justified. SPs procrastinate and often hate work in which they find no joy. They often work hard as artisans or musicians, not so much for the sake of performance but for the joy of creating. SPs may struggle with low self–esteem, prompted by judging SJs and a complementary belief that God is probably an SJ.

For SPs surrender may mean giving up this irresponsible image and being the deeper self God is calling them to be—being faithful to relationships with God and others and committed to a spiritual path. Surrender involves taking the bad days—as well as the good days—as a gift from God. Deep surrender may deliver them from low self–esteem, as they find their identity in an affirming God. SPs can savor the quality of life and presence of God as no other temperament can.

Saint Francis was an SP. Before surrender, he lived for the moment, spending his father's money. But as he flung off this identity and his fancy clothes, he identified with Jesus as the poor man in love with lady poverty.

Intuitive–feeling types (NFs) are idealistic and adventurous, enthusiastic and imaginative. They enjoy people and have a deep need to be appreciated. They enjoy getting to know a new person, learning new things, discovering new places.

They may become workaholics, not so much out of duty as out of fascination with a goal. They may become addicted to helping, fixing, and "relating," because "ordinary" life is so dull. They can be blind to what needs to be done, even while looking over the landscape for new projects. NFPs may prefer starting a new project then have trouble finishing it or meeting the deadline. NFJs may be driven to finish.

For some NFs superficiality and small talk may be painful. Their self–image may thrive on being popular, enthusiastic, and inspirational.

Their approach to life may be romantic or poetic— not based in reality. They may work hard to make their mark but suffer depression because they are not meeting their own unrealistically high goals.

NFs may feel that God wants more of them; if they are dissatisfied with themselves, God must feel the same toward them. This may play into a toxic shame or an obsession with neurotic guilt. They can be overwhelmed by small problems because they see them as the sign of their failure. NFs may fear living with limits and being fallible and human.

For the NF surrender means letting go of false dreams, so God can be found in the ordinary and real. Surrender may involve finding a balanced optimism, basking in the affirmation of the God who loves them just as they are. It is possible for a redeemed NF to love deeply and inspire others to do the same.

An NF, Saint Augustine resisted giving up the adventure of unchastity and his lack of focus in theology. But in surrender he responded to and found his rest in God's love.

Intuitive–thinking types (NTs) are independent and analytical and often wind up in teaching or some aspect of design. Wanting to verify everything for themselves, they tend to be skeptical of what others tell them. They may be the most creative and resourceful of all types. If there is a better way of doing something, they will find it. But they think their way is the best way.

It is difficult for NTs to let go and let others or God do things. They can be harshly critical of anyone who is not as efficient or effective as they are. They can be impatient with group processes—any slow process.

Fearing stupidity and inconsistency—even in themselves—NTs try to control processes or people. They may see God as judging and critical, the master designer who disdains stupidity. This means they can shut themselves off from grace and from others and from their own feelings.

Surrender may involve seeing the mystery and irrationality of life— in themselves, in others, and in life in the larger sense. If NTs can seek values along with logic, they may be able to communicate their magnificent insights without alienating their audience. They may find their way to the God of truth and stand in awe as they surrender their need to be God.

As an NT, C. S. Lewis came to God as "the most miserable convert in all England," because it was hard for him to admit that God was God.

But his redeemed imagination and playfulness led him to write children's stories and science fiction. After his wife died, his anger turned to passionate writing about his grief.

These patterns of struggle and surrender may not seem to fit for some people. The exercises at the end of the chapter might seem artificial. If they see just one area in which God is calling them to "let go" and surrender, then that is the area for them to concentrate on and pray about.

If some are blithely unaware of God's call toward a more centered life, they might pray for an awareness of that call. They might pray for the grace to say yes to God. The emphasis is not on our surrender but on God's grace. And God always is willing to give us a new measure of grace.

Those familiar with the twelve steps might "rework" the first three steps. I see them as the one–two–three dance that puts us in God's arms. It might be once again committing one's life to Jesus Christ as Lord and Savior. In what area is Jesus not number one? In what areas is our self–image based on feelings or self–doubts rather than on God's gracious forgiveness in Christ?

Notes for Leaders

•   Work on this material depends on people understanding the content of the material on temperaments presented in the previous chapter.

•   *Small–group sessions.* I distribute the "Temperament as a Focus for a Centered Life" handout, printed at the end of this chapter. This exercise may be difficult for some. Start with the basic understanding that our character needs to be reformed, with God at the center. If you can, give an example of surrender from your own life.

Explain that the MBTI gives some clues about the particular kind of character transformation God may be up to. On a flipchart or blackboard, you might show how many people in the group place themselves in each of the four temperaments. To illustrate that each temperament involves a different weakness and different kind of surrender, you might refer to the parable of the sower—seeds falling on different types of ground.

Give people permission to work through the exercises on their own. The goal is to have them put into words *one* area that needs to be surrendered—a grace to beg for, an idea that may set them free. *Beg* is the term used by Ignatius. It reminds us to ask passionately for what we desire.

Some people do better just writing about: "What area of your life do you think God is trying to change? Where are you trying to control what you can't What are you not taking responsibility for?"

After the exercise, people may break into groups of two (having the same temperament) for discussion. If discussion doesn't "come," suggest they read and think about the exercise again later and ask God for light.

A second handout, "Worksheet: My Practice," might be given for people to complete before the final Beginning Again session.

Temperament as a Focus for a Centered Life

Review the characteristics of your temperament type and look at the "Controlling and Graceful Images" chart below. Then work through this exercise with an open mind and an open heart. What is God saying? What grace is God wanting to give you? Take time to write your responses.

Controlling and Graceful Images of Self and God

	Controlling self-image	Graceful self-image	Controlling image of God	Graceful image of God
SJ	is overly responsible	accept limits	demanding giver	freedom
SP	avoids pain	enjoys life	wants pain	joy giver
NF	is romantic	is hopeful realist	dissatisfied	love giver
NT	is harshly skeptical	is insightful	judging	truth giver

Questions for SJs

1. In the description of the SJ temperament, what do you recognize that fits you?

2. Can you recognize in the description one or more areas you need to surrender? What would they be?

3. What image of God from scripture, music, or your own experience liberates you from your characteristic sin? If God were your liberator, what would God free you from? What can you do to help you keep in mind the image of God as your liberator?

4. What truth from God would set you free?

5. What grace—that comes as a gift—do you need to beg for? What power? Attitude? Could it be the grace of surrender, the delight of receiving?

6. What daily practice might you use to help you when you revert to the control and subsequent lack of freedom that is easy for you to "fall into," considering your temperament? Might it be a song, maybe "Nothing in my hands I bring, solely to thy cross I cling"?

Questions for SPs

1. In the description of the SP temperament, what do you recognize that fits you?

2. Can you recognize in the description one or more areas you need to surrender? What would they be?

3. What healing image of God comes to you from scripture or music or your own experience? Consider the generous God of Jesus and Saint Francis.

4. Can you identify the saving truth that frees you from your compulsion? What would it be?

5. What daily practice might you use to help you when you revert to the

control and subsequent lack of freedom that is easy for you to "fall into," considering your temperament? Does breathing out tension and fear help you be here in the present?

Questions for NFs

1. In the description of the NF temperament, what do you recognize that fits you?

2. Can you recognize in the description one or more areas you need to surrender? What would they be?

3. What image of God from scripture, music, or your own experience liberates you from your characteristic sin? How do you know God as lover?

4. What truth from God would set you free?

5. What grace—that comes as a gift you cannot earn but may receive—do you need to beg for? Might it be the grace to receive the truth?

6. What daily practice might you use to help you when you revert to the control and subsequent lack of freedom that is easy for you to "fall into," considering your temperament? Does practicing the presence of God help you find God in the ordinary?

Questions for NTs

1. In the description of the NT temperament, what do you recognize that fits you?

2. Do you agree with the need for surrender? What do you know you need to surrender?

3. What image of God from scripture or music or your own experience helps liberate you?

4. What grace do you need to beg for—God's gift to you? Might it be the grace or gift of accepting human imperfection?

5. What daily practice might you use to help you when you are "caught" being less than perfect? Might it be one of the twelve steps: I "came to believe that a Power greater than [myself] could restore [me] to sanity"?

Questions for Everyone to Consider

1. What are the priorities of your life? Place them in order of importance.

2. Where is God calling you? In what direction are you moving?

3. How do these priorities become aligned with the intention of God—that you love God with all your heart, soul, mind, and strength, and that you love your neighbor as yourself?

4. The gospel song "Amazing Grace" says, "Tis grace that brought me safe thus far, and grace will lead me home." Is this true for you? Where is home?

You may want to take these questions home to work on and pray over.

Worksheet: My Practice

1. Having prayed for light about God's intention for me, having searched my heart for my deepest need, at this moment I see that my priorities for living are:
   a.
   b.
   c.

2. As I understand the call of God, it is to:

3. As I understand God's invitation to surrender, to grow, it is in this primary area:

4. This is what I want to do:

5. This is what I need to let go of:

6. This is the program or practice I need to keep on track, to be in daily touch with God:

	Daily	Weekly	Monthly	Yearly
Prayer				
Meditation				
Inventory				
Support from				

7. If this seems overwhelming, what one thing can I do faithfully to listen to God?

CHAPTER 7

Ending and Beginning Again

When God created us, God gave Adam a secret—and that secret was not how to begin, but how to begin again.

In other words, it is not given to us to begin; that privilege is God's alone. But it is given to us to begin again—and we do every time we choose to defy death and side with the living.[1]

—Elie Wiesel, who began again

Always rise up with fresh courage. I am glad you make a fresh beginning daily; there is no better means of attaining to the spiritual life than by continually beginning again.[2]

—Jean Pierre Camus

At the end of this program, we find an opportunity to begin—a new, more intentional relationship with God.

In one sense, we begin again every morning when we choose consciously to orient ourselves toward God. We begin again every time we pick ourselves up after stumbling. We begin again when we turn to God after hours or days of not being aware of God's presence. We begin again when we keep to our discipline, our faithful effort to let God love us. We begin again when we realize one path leads to isolation and ill health, another leads to life.

We can solidify the gains in awareness made in this program by writing a mission statement. If this sounds too trendy, consider writing a statement of what you are about right now.

I can remember the difference in my life when I decided that God was more important than my work. That insight may seem elementary, especially for a clergyman. But it is difficult *especially* for clergy; if we think our work is for God, it quickly can *become* our god.

At midlife I found myself working too hard, not emotionally present to my wife and children, and struggling to make a little time for conscious contact with God. But I decided that my relationship with God was first, that my soul's nurture was my first responsibility. I also decided that my family was in second place, before my work. I wish I had made this decision years earlier. My children might have had better fathering, and my wife, more of the husband's love she deserved. On my deathbed, I will *not* wish I had worked more. Yet I frequently wish I had been there more for my wife and children. If I had, I would have in turn been a better person and a better pastor. I also wish I had been more intentional about friends outside my work setting.

Taking a week's retreat five years ago also offered enormous help in deciding what to do with my life. Until that point I was worried about making money, worried about future possibilities for employment. Career can be idolatry. But on retreat, after hearing God's love for me, I was able to hear the call of God: to help people grow spiritually. The place was immaterial. The details would unfold. I didn't get an outline but a direction—and that deeply fulfilled me.

Consider writing a mission statement that is realistic. Don't set impossible, inflexible goals. Try to include a form of accountability and spiritual support. I see having an intentional relationship with God as being like climbing the Himalayas. Anyone can stroll in the foothills. But beyond that point, you usually need a guide and helpmates to carry the food. To make it to the top, you need to rope yourself together to your guide. Who will you look to for support and spiritual guidance?

Then periodically reevaluate your goals and your support system. My own mission statement looks like this:

• To love God and receive God's grace. To care for myself in exercise, with friends, and in daily prayer.

• To love my wife, children, mother, and friends, and to spend quality time with them in a mutual and interdependent relationship.

• To help people grow spiritually.

•   To be faithful to this, I will share this with at least one support group and will at least ten times a year meet with my spiritual director. I will share my resistance to prayer and share where I think God is calling me to grow.

•   I will be in two support groups where I am not the leader.

•   I will be open and mutually disclosing to at least two friends about the issues of my spirituality.

•   I will do an examen daily, spend one day a month to more carefully align myself to God's love, and a week a year in retreat.

Your mission statement isn't a standard that you "must" measure up to. Let it stretch you but not break you and leave you in despair if you don't meet your goals.

This series is about Beginning Again—not about giving up.

Notes for Leaders

•   *In small groups.* If group participants are centered and reasonably emotionally healthy, ask them to divide into groups of two. Have one ask the other repeatedly for two minutes, "What do you really want?"

Or you might lead a guided imagery, where Jesus asks participants three times, "What do you want?" Then have participants ask Jesus three times, "What do you want?"

For participants interested in continuing to pursue a vital relationship with God, I use the handout "My Habits for Spiritual Growth." The "Worksheet" handout at the end of chapter 6 helps prepare participants for writing a personal mission statement. This is hard for many people to do individually. Having people working alone but in a room where others are also writing can provide support to the process.

At the end of the Beginning Again program, I ask participants for an evaluation and some sort of commitment about what they will do next. Questions include (1) How helpful did you find the time together? (2) How could it have been improved? (3) What is the next step for you? Do you need help from the church?

Most participants will be praying more than they were at the beginning of the course. Many will have started a daily practice that they intend to maintain. But many will get out of the habit of daily prayer and this will lead to depression or guilt. I try to forestall this by reading the quotes at the beginning of this chapter.

My Habits for Spiritual Growth

Center, breathe, ask for the gift of guidance.

1. If Jesus were to ask you right now, "[Your name], what do you want?" what would you say?

2. Listen to Jesus calling you now. Where does he beckon you to go? What does he beckon you to be or do?

3. Write out a statement of your priorities or a mission statement. Perhaps you would like to include goals for every area of your life: your relationship with God; your relationship with a significant other; relationships with friends; your work; your self care. Is there a symbol— a story, a scripture passage—that expresses your goal? What are you moving from? Toward?
   Consider that Jesus said our first mission was to love God; our second was to love our neighbor. How does your purpose or mission get aligned with the great purposes of God?

4. What can you do daily and weekly that will remind you of your unique mission? How can you tell if you are faithful to the mission and headed in the right direction? What do you need from others to help you on your way?

Daily:

Weekly:

Monthly:

Yearly:

PART TWO

For the Parish Leadership: Theology and Attitude

I'd like to define three levels of spiritual guidance. Though the three overlap at times, the important distinctions are based on the purpose of the relationship and the training and competence of the guide. All three types of guidance can be given by laypeople or clergy. I owe the classifications to Gerald May.[1]

Spiritual formation. Used widely in many circles, this term involves helping form a person's spirituality, character, and spiritual practice.

This happens in homes and parishes, with friends, as well as in classes and seminaries. It includes imparting ideas, giving examples, being in community.

Almost anyone can provide spiritual formation. The ones who do it well have their own faith, their own spiritual life, nourished by another person or group. This quality provides the unique character of Roman Catholic schools, Quaker communities, and many homes.

Spiritual companionship. This is a more intentional process of helping people pay attention to God. It is at the core of the Beginning Again course. It is what evangelicals call "discipling." It is what should happen in seminary but usually doesn't. It is more than teaching; it is helping people pay attention to the reality of God and respond to God. It is not about ideas but love, not beliefs but faith.

Spiritual direction. This is a formal, one–on–one relationship that focuses on one person's relationship with God. Two people meet regularly, usually monthly. As a rule the director has been trained in the art of guidance and personal development, is being supervised, and is in direction her/himself.

The term *spiritual direction* bothers some people. The guidance is not spiritual in opposition to psychological or physical; rather, the focus is on the Spirit of God. And it is not *direction* in a hierarchical manner; it is trying to discern what direction the Holy Spirit is giving. The Spirit, God working in us, is the true director. Spiritual direction is discerning that reality. Direction is not friendship alone for it may include precision in discernment, confrontation, and offering specific suggestions.

In the context of this book, I suggest that pastors should be spiritual companions and train lay leaders to be spiritual companions. I believe every pastor should be in spiritual direction and have some guidance in learning how to be a companion to parishioners. Lay leaders of groups should have received some companionship help as well as supervision in leading small groups.

Pastors need not and probably should not be trained as spiritual directors and should not be spiritual directors for parishioners. To lead companionship groups, laypeople need not be trained as spiritual directors. They may be spiritual directors, but they are probably wise not to direct friends and co–workers in their own small parishes. In very large parishes this may be all right.

CHAPTER 8

Corporate Spirituality

How does the Spirit of God infuse and animate a congregation or a group? How can leaders encourage an average group or a parish to notice God's hand at work, to be what God intends?

Jesus prayed:

> The goal is for all of them to become one heart and mind--
> Just as you, Father, are in me and I in you (John 17:21 TM).

> Then they'll be mature in this oneness,
> And give the godless world evidence
> That you've sent me and loved them
> In the same way that you've loved me (John 17:23 TM).

Jesus' prayer is quite radical; he asks that the same quality of oneness and communion–love that is his and the Father's be in the church. I believe this is not doctrinal or sacramental or organizational unity but the unity of love, of relationship.

Many books have been written about individual spiritual life. One can buy lots of books about church or small–group leadership. There are several about renewal of a parish—centering on spiritual awakening on the part of individual members or quality management. But I haven't seen many encouraging the development of love in management and in members, of spiritual awakening in a normal parish.

What can we do to foster this? First, we can pay attention to the unity, the community, the love, the presence of God that is already there.

Paying Attention

For several years early in my ministry, I served as chaplain in a psychiatric hospital, where I ran religious discussion and worship groups. These were usually on locked wards, with patients who showed some promise of contact with others. After discussing some issue of importance to the patients, I would lead a worship service drawing on the issues we had talked about. Some days these seemed to "jell"; people asked powerful questions and listened to one another; the words for our worship period fitted the reality of what we had done. On other days I had all the right words, but the emotional or spiritual reality didn't seem to be there. Even worse, some days the reality of our being with each other seemed to be profound, but worship seemed dead. One day over lunch a bright colleague said, "Some days it's just the words; other times it's the music (spirit); and some days they go together gloriously!" Yes. Words and music. Word and Spirit.

The music of the Spirit is not ours to give, but we can at least notice, pray for, and be open to the gentle breeze of the Spirit. The Spirit of God prays within us "with sighs too deep for words" (Rom. 8:26). Even when we are unaware of it, our sighs and breaths are prayers of surrender and invocation. Theologian Paul Tillich says this about the sighs deeper than words: "Words, created by and used in our conscious life, are not the essence of prayer. The essence of prayer is the act of God who is working in us and raises our whole being to himself."[1]

There is a big difference between saying the words and the underlying meaning or attitude. David Steindl-Rast, a Benedictine monk known worldwide for his wisdom, says:

> We must distinguish prayer from prayerfulness.... Prayerfulness is an attitude of the heart.... There is no human heart that does not pray, at least in deep dreams that nourish life with meaning. Moments in which we drink deeply from the source of meaning are moments of prayer, whether we call them so or not.[2]

Our task is to pay attention, to listen, to be prayed through. But most churches have so emphasized getting the words of liturgy right, the theology right, the action in the right direction that we haven't paid attention to the spiritual reality the words were supposed to point to.

So the first thing we can do is to pay attention to our hearts, to the prayer that is already happening. The second thing we can do is to pay attention to the group, the Spirit's corporate dimension.

Discern Group Spirituality

Before we get into specifics about how to encourage the Spirit, we must ask another question. How do we see the interrelationships among person and church and Spirit?

The church setting may encourage or discourage individual formation. And the spirituality of leaders will affect the climate of the group. The climate, the economy, the history of the group will also affect the group. And their receptiveness will affect the leaders.

I think of God, the individual, and the group as a complex web of interrelationships. We can use traditional systems descriptions to get at this with diagrams and charts. Or we can be more imaginative and think of the character, the personality, the spirit or "angel" of a group. I take this term from the book of Revelation, which refers to the angel of various first–century congregations.

Is there a unique corporate spirituality, an attitude toward God in a group? Yes, as apparent as the character of an institution or family or individual. Sensitive people may pick much of this up right away. This character may be positive or negative, formed by the spirit's moving or by dysfunction. A group's spirituality may be organized around shame in the case of clergy abuse or financial dishonesty. A normal parish may be organized around religious nostalgia. Or the group may be focused on the experience of the living God.

My present parish puzzled me at first. At first the people seemed like "American Gothic," rather rigid and reserved. Their practices seemed to be on another planet from the three-thousand-member congregation I had moved from. These parishioners and I had lived in the same large metropolitan area for years, but the character of the parish seemed radically different from my style and values.

One day a college–student visitor commented that spiritually we belonged in a small town in the country, maybe even in the mythical Lake Wobegon of Garrison Keillor fame. Yes, that was it. We were a small town in a major metropolis. This spirit involved a lack of sophistication in some areas and a genuine sense of community and openness that was one of our strengths. After I adjusted my expectations to what the church was, this church felt like "home," like the first church I'd pastored or the church I had grown up in.

But it wasn't just church size and identity that I picked up on, it was our style of spirituality. That style is characterized by the matriarchs and patriarchs speaking openly about their ideas or feelings, listening to the differences, and after voting getting on with it. Because these people are so secure, they are open to others who hold different beliefs and practice, providing the parishioners get to know these people individually. We aren't concerned with political correctness on the left or the right spectrum. The church is open to inviting newcomers to lead. In medium to large churches, people often argue about issues like feminism. Our tradition is that we usually don't discuss issues so much as respond to people. One of our new elders wanted inclusive language, and some young, female worship leaders have used feminine language about God. In response, there may have been some gritting of teeth and shifting of gears, but because the congregation knew these people, there was no argument or backlash. When the denominational report on homosexuality came out, I gave my point of view and asked others for theirs. From nine session members, we had nine different points of view. We didn't argue about what was right. We simply acknowledged that there were at least several points of view.

The spirituality of my parish grows out of our geography and sociology and history but is rooted in our experience of God. The parishioners were open to practically anything I did in a worship service, since the liturgical forms weren't important to them. But remembering their history, the memorial gifts given, their veterans and prior service of leaders—these things were very important. So were the devotional booklets passed out each month. When these were not available, I sensed considerable consternation.

We may think of the spirit of a group or person as the inside, that which is within, the inner truth. This is not just a metaphor, but the relationship, the character, the quality of the group or person. Walter Wink does a great job of discussing this in his book *Engaging the Powers*.[3]

These "starter" questions might help you discern the corporate spirituality of your congregation: (1) What do the climate, the weather, the lakes, or mountains say about the spirit of the area? (2) What is the nature of this part of the country, state, or city? (3) What is the history of this parish, the style of your being together? (4) What is your recent parish history? (5) How are you different from other parishes? (6) What is the current spirit of your congregation? (7) How do you see yourselves? (8) Is there an image, picture, or person that might symbolize the group? (9) Can you draw a picture or give a symbol of an animal that symbolizes the group? (10) For your congregation is there an "angel"—a personification of your corporate spirituality? (11) Is there a dark side? (12) Who gives you feedback from outside the community? Do you ask newcomers? Have you hired a consultant to learn from an outsider's point of view? (13) Where is God nudging you? Where is God present in your midst?

A Business Viewpoint

Management consultant Stephen Covey encourages spirituality another way. He urges people and corporations to have a mission statement, not just goals. Covey doesn't mention the word spirituality and gives only a small hint in the appendix about his religious affiliation. Yet I believe that Covey's book *The Seven Habits of Highly Effective People* is highly spiritual and may be readily translated from business into the local church.

Covey says that the mission statement for people and organizations should be oriented to universal principles and unique to every individual, family, work group, or corporation. These principles should be greater than making money or satisfying a person's ego. Such a mission statement, even in a secular, business setting, might be seen as identifying a corporate spirituality.

Covey also says that we need to think about our mission using both sides of our brains. We need pictures and stories as well as principles. We need poetic pictures and rational sentences. This is spirit and soul together.

How do Christians and churches get at an image of mission, think about corporate spirituality? Churches have sounded like corporations recently—while Covey talks to business as if it were a church.

The Role of the Pastor

According to Eugene Peterson the last one hundred years have seen a major shift in the role of pastor. In earlier centuries the pastor during the week studied scripture, had conversations with parishioners about their spiritual lives, and prayed. Now pastors don't do much, if any of these activities, because they are managing or running a parish. Roman Catholic priests celebrate the sacraments and manage the money. Evangelicals may study scripture, but they don't help people in their prayer lives. Liberal pastors help people adjust to life, and prayer may be one of the means. But few pastors have an interest in what used to be called the care or cure of souls.

Though he doesn't use the word, I see more spirituality in Covey's *Seven Habits* than in most clergy journals. Why? Because Covey says the job of leaders is to have a mission that ties into eternal principles. He urges leaders to hold themselves accountable on a weekly basis to how they live up to personal and corporate mission statements.

It might be revolutionary if a congregation's and a pastor's mission statements included "helping parishioners increase their love for God and others." This—not numbers or "feeling good"—would be the bottom line to measure activity.

A Biblical Vision of Corporate Spirituality

The divine pattern of ultimate reality is the loving relationship of the Trinity: Father, Son, and Holy Ghost; Creator, Redeemer, Sanctifier; Earth-Maker, Pain-Bearer, Life-giver.[4]

This pattern gives us a clue, says H. A. Williams, Anglican member of the Community of the Resurrection, for solving one of our oldest problems: How can we be in relationships without being absorbed by our needs or by the other person?

We fall in love and have a fleeting and false sense of union. But then the romance stops, and a power struggle starts. Then we may become isolated. With a newborn child we may experience an initial sense of togetherness. But children grow up and leave. Again and again we have a taste of union, to be followed by periods of anger or power struggles or loneliness. As one of my friends says, we want intimacy until we get scared of being too close or suffocated by the other. We move away until we feel out of the loop, out of the relationship.

But the Trinity models intimacy and uniqueness, community with interrelationships. The Holy Trinity is the mysterious community of God; God invites the church to be transformed into such a community.

The classical pattern, says Calvin, is "Union, not fusion; distinction, not separation." That sounds very academic and dead. C. S. Lewis puts this in an equally orthodox but more playful way:

> In Christianity God is not a static thing--not even a person--but a dynamic, pulsating activity, a life, almost a kind of drama. Almost, if you will not think me irreverent, a kind of dance. The union between the Father and the Son is such a live concrete thing that this union itself is a person....
>
> The whole dance, or drama, or pattern of this three–Personal life is to be played out in each one of us: or each one of us has got to enter that pattern, take his place in that dance.[5]

This requires contemplation of God, paying attention to the images of scripture and imagination where God is revealed to us. Contemplation, not theology. Contemplation, not ethics. Contemplation in action, thinking, feeling.

God's love for us, inviting us to join the dance of God, is the fulfillment of the prayer of Jesus for the church: unity like that he knew with the Father.

So then our prayer, our loves, our relationships—oriented toward God—will have this pattern. They will be respectful, joyful, changing, mutual. They will be interdependent. That is just the opposite of most relationships in family and church, which involve hierarchy, anarchy, boredom, rigidity, and a lack of mutuality.

God Invites Us to Change

We are invited to move from total dependence as a child to this interdependence, this dance of the Trinity. Leaving one stage for the next will feel like death. I heard of a lecturer on child and adult development who piled up blocks, explaining that this is the way we like to think of growth –one stage building on another. But, she said as she wiped all the blocks off the table to the floor, this is how it feels. At a new stage everything is gone, and we start from scratch again. This is why adolescence is so painful, and why most people don't want to change or grow after that. Typically at middle age, life again throws the pile on the floor.

Spiritual direction gives the insight that God is always working in our lives, and our job is to pay attention. Sometimes God moves in helping us put things together; more often, God is in the process of change and growth. Ignatius said he wasn't surprised when he was directing people and found rage and joy, tears or massive resistance. He found unrelenting cheerfulness a state in which he could not recognize the Spirit. God is out to make people anew, growing, becoming more who they really are. In Romans 12:2, Paul said, "Fix your attention on God. You'll be changed from the inside out" (TM). We need to be making new wineskins for new wine, as Jesus said in Luke 5:38.

Just when I think we've finally got something in place in the parish, along comes a new family with a new perspective. Or, in my prayer life, in comes a new way of seeing the darkness within me and a new invitation to turn to God and surrender something else. There is continual conversion, not for the sake of change, but for the sake of God.

Corporate spirituality? You bet. God is making all things new: congregations and small groups and individual people. We know we are interrelated and interdependent when we wake up to reality. But I believe that we need to notice the Spirit at two levels at once, deeply inside each one of us and corporately, in our common life together.

We are being danced through, prayed through, by the living God.

Implications for the Local Church

The vision is first. Without a vision the people perish in the parish. Or they are bored and need constant stimulation of new programs as though it were religious entertainment. We need a vision of the character of who God is and of who we are meant to be. As the leadership listens to God and discerns the mission, hierarchical models and individualistic understandings of being church will have to change.

In my present parish there was a potentially divisive situation when we doubled the membership within several years and replaced most of the old leadership. But a new couple suggested "supper circles," each including old and new members. Enjoying food and fellowship, people told parts of their stories. There is a growing respect between new and old, between the generations. I later read this as a suggestion for renewing old congregations, allowing the newcomers to hear the stories of the oldtimers and vice versa.

We also stumbled on to the idea of writing a mission statement and hired a consultant to help us do this. It has helped both the oldtimers and the newcomers find our common purpose, and it continues to guide our programming and budgeting. We evaluate ourselves not in the light of money or numbers as much as whether we have done and been what we think God has intended for us. Some congregations go nuts evaluating themselves. We don't. We print out our mission and ask people and groups to evaluate the pastor, the leadership group, their group, and themselves personally and to identify where the growing edge might be. When there is a general consensus, great. Any significant differences are an opportunity to share perspectives.

Here is our mission statement:

> Bryn Mawr Presbyterian Church is
> a welcoming Christian community
> developing personal relationships with God,
> growing together in love and faith, and
> promoting social responsibility.

The parish leaders have owned the statement and the ministry, and I am not the center of leadership. My role is more to ask questions and to point out where I sense God is leading us.

The mission statement is one of the best ways to change the direction of a parish. It is like turning the rudder on a supertanker. Many times pastors and leaders try to push the bow of a ship to force the congregation to change. That way only brings more resistance. To work on the rudder together may seem to be insignificant. But if the leadership believes it and measures itself in the light of the mission, there is profound and continued change. But to do that the leaders must have a vision that comes from God. In what direction is God calling? "The Spirit, not content to flit around on the surface, dives into the depths of God" (1 Cor. 2:10 TM).

Leadership is dependent upon inner spiritual growth and psychological development. Leaders need to be rooted and grounded in love, in faith, in vision, in principles, or they will lead a deformed group. They will want to be program managers or fixers rather than pastors. A friend of mine suggested I read Eugene Peterson, pastor of one church for more than thirty years. Peterson is a prophet to pastors, as he says:

> The pastors of America have metamorphosed into a company of shopkeepers and the shops they keep are churches. They are preoccupied with shopkeepers' concerns--how to keep customers happy, how to lure customers away from competitors down the street, how to package the goods so that the customers will lay out more money.... The pastor's responsibility is to keep the community attentive to God. It is this responsibility that is being abandoned in spades.[6]

The parish will worship idols rather than the living God:

> Why do pastors have such a difficult time in being pastors? Because we are awash in idolatry.... The idolatry to which pastors are conspicuously liable is not personal but vocational, the idolatry of a religious career....
>
> Vocational holiness, in deliberate opposition to career idolatry, is my subject.[7]

> The paradigm shift that I am after is from pastor as program director to pastor as spiritual director.[8]

Pastors and leaders will need their own personal mission statements and their own regular discipline to get in touch with God's dream for their ministry. To do this most need a support group and an individual mentor.

Unless they have relationships outside the church and denomination, leaders are usually captured by their parochial culture, codependent and overly subject to the expectations of the in-group. Before leaders can see to preach prophetically (take the specks, the idolatry, out of their congregations' eyes), they need help in taking the log out of their own. Leaders need support groups that can give them feedback and help them see the projections they make on the members of the groups they're leading.

To be rooted and grounded in love, leaders responsible for others' spiritual growth need one-on-one mentoring or spiritual direction. This support is not therapy; it involves being realigned in the direction of the Spirit. Leaders also need to know something about patterns of adult development and individual differences, or else they will tend to think everyone is just like them.

Group growth requires individual growth. For the whole group to grow, every individual needs help to get in touch with his or her own individuality in God. How is God manifest at the core of my being? This recognition of the individual is seriously resisted by most hierarchical churches that are used to controlling theology, process, and programs.

In the less hierarchical and more egalitarian systems of church government, only the Society of Friends (Quakers) have cherished individuality and corporate discernment. For the rest, the issue is usually not "what is God's will?" but "who has the votes?" And when this doesn't work, a consultant comes in to give advice on process. This is an organizational fix, not encouraging individual people to grow and deepen.

For the group and individual to be aligned with God's purposes, the group together needs to listen to God, to compare its spirit to the Holy Spirit. This may be called group inventory or group discernment and is more than an evaluation of work at the end of the year. At least the governing board and congregation need to look at what has been done and compare it against the mission statement. The congregation should have a series of questions that it wrestles with so that it can examine its life by the truth. It is good to have written questions that encourage awareness of both light and shadow in leaders and in groups. "You're blessed when you get your inside world--your mind and heart--put right. Then you can see God in the outside world" (Matt. 5:8 TM).

A group discernment process should not be limited to the spiritual elite who want to gather in exclusive groups with their like-minded colleagues. The process of discernment should be done throughout the congregation in working and fellowship groups. In our church's evangelism committee, we talk about what God is doing in our lives. How can we offer the gospel to outsiders if God isn't real for us? In the stewardship committee, we talk about the spirituality of money, and how our hearts and priorities are affected by giving. Even for our fall cleanup, we usually gather around the piano at the end of the day and sing a few gospel songs. Adult education isn't just talking about scripture; it's helping people read the scripture and listen to and discern God's word addressed to them. Theology is seen as a roadmap to God. Our focus is not on the map but the journey. In children's education, we try to listen to them to see what God is doing in their lives. The choir not only provides music as performance but helps people pray.

There is a natural desire to isolate "spirituality" into a separate function. To do so kills the effectiveness of the Spirit, as does limiting religion to Sunday morning. Encouraging everyone in the church to be exposed to some kind of spiritual process changes the whole church system and the way individual members think of themselves.

Perhaps the most leverage to change the attitude toward the Spirit comes on Sunday morning. In our parish we have been including more laypeople as leaders in the morning worship service. Not being religious professionals, their presence and witness is noticed. Allowing silence in the service and thus encouraging private prayer may initially be resisted. "Bidding prayers," where the leader suggests an area of prayer and then prays a collect after the silence can be effective. Some Episcopal churches sing Taizé songs before the formal worship begins. We sing popular responses throughout the service. We have people tell their stories directly or indirectly through a children's story before the service begins. We light candles before the service as people ask for specific prayers for themselves or others.

Some results of these Sunday morning patterns? Now in committee meetings people will ask for prayer, and when I visit homes, many people will say a surprisingly open prayer of grace.

I am fairly disclosing of my needs and my spiritual journey. I find that times of discouragement or deadness are especially good to share, because people usually hear only positive prayers and heroic stories. Knowing that consolation and desolation—ups and downs—are part of the spiritual journey is very helpful for many.

Group discernment is more effective through personal inventory. Group discernment is generally more effective if leaders and members have a regular practice of personal inventory, of examination of consciousness, of obeying Paul who says: "Examine yourselves. . . . Do you not realize that Christ is in you?" (2 Cor. 13:5). For some this is a weekly "sharpening of the saw," measuring time and energy spent against their vision statement. For others it is a daily reading of scripture, not for ideas but for the personal truth that reorients and corrects us.

Ignatius of Loyola says that discernment of God begins with principles, but moves to noticing the movements within oneself. Finally it means being able to discern which of the inner movements are from God and which are not. This kind of spiritual maturity is needed by the leaders if the congregation is to mature.

Family systems can benefit from inventory. Many leaders can benefit from personal work in family systems, looking at their family of origin, possibly by constructing a genogram. All of us resort to childish or defensive reactions when attacked, and stirring up resistance and resentment is a natural consequence of leadership. When I grow defensive or resentful with people in the parish or group, it is almost always a reflection of a blind spot I have because of my family story and old patterns of relating that are no longer appropriate. Paul Tillich says,

> In pathological cases, psychotherapy is needed.... But more is needed, namely the dependence on that which gives ultimate independence...in God, the inescapable conflicts of every family are overcome.[9]

When I can quickly look at my defensiveness prayerfully, I can see what is going on and ask God for help and healing. I am at least able to separate my emotional reaction from God's will.

Leaders help groups discern the leading of God. Leaders are encouraged to ask where the call or leading of God is—both in internal spiritual movements and in external circumstances. Many people adequately solve problems, but leaders should help congregations or groups past problem solving—to the place where they can notice the activity of God in a given situation. Before this can be done with the congregation, the leader should have been attentive to the inner movement of the Spirit in his life on a daily basis, guided by a codiscerning group or individual. Prophetic leaders may see the call of God in disaster, and charismatic leaders may feel God in warm feelings and numerical success. The great leader is the one who can help discern God in both of these movements as well as in the ordinary.

Finally, we may be able to see God in all relationships, in everything, calling us to change our dance as the music changes, being danced through, animated, by the music of the Trinity, the Earth-Maker, Pain-Bearer, and Life-Giver.

CHAPTER 9

Leadership

The model we have for community in the New Testament and in the Trinity is interdependency: a dance, an intimate relationship of mutuality—joyful, changing, respectful, inclusive. The Trinity is community with interrelationships; union without fusion; distinction without separation.

This is the opposite of how we live in our families and churches, where the model is typically mutual dependency or codependency, with precious little joy or freedom.

Clergyman Frederick Buechner is pessimistic about his experiences with the local congregation:

> The church often bears an uncomfortable resemblance to the dysfunctional family. There is the authoritarian presence of the minister–the professional who knows all of the answers and calls most of the shots--whom few ever challenge either because they don't dare or because they feel it wouldn't do any good if they did. Then there is the outward camaraderie and inward loneliness of the congregation, the doubts and discouragements that for propriety's sake are kept more or less under cover.[1]

I see variations of this. I see pastors acting out in destructive ways and parishes wanting to get rid of their pastors. I see churches dominated by dysfunctional laity who bully the pastors and the rest of the leaders. Clergy either overreact, developing all kinds of illness, or leave. Most denominations don't have well–trained consultants to intervene or exert some external authority.

Even in parishes considered normal or healthy, I see precious little that passes for real spiritual transformation. When successful pastors come to my course most of them are very limited developmentally; most cannot model or coach spiritual maturity for parishioners. Their churches are filled with good programs for every conceivable cause, but parishioners are not being rooted and grounded in God's love.

More books or seminars won't fix this. We need new ways of acting and being that come from Christ within. How do we change the patterns of relationships in our parishes?

One way is to think about what is wrong. Paul, in his study of leadership in 2 Corinthians, calls the world "unprincipled" (2 Cor. 10:3 TM). And such ego-centered people concerned with survival at any price come into the church.

Let's look for some answers to the question "What is wrong?"

Three Ways of Looking at Leadership

The body. One answer is found in the image of the head and the body. It's the image Rabbi Edwin Friedman uses to talk about family systems as they apply to the church. Friedman says that the clergy is the head of the body of the congregation, and if the head is not differentiated from the rest of the body, it will not do its job. What does he mean by differentiation? He sees many leaders who can stay in touch with the rest of the organization; a few, he says, can become independent of the body of believers; only a very few—those who are differentiated—can be independent *and* in touch. If the leader is differentiated, the rest of the organization is not dominated by the most dependent member. Rather, the organization and everyone in it is able to function more freely and independently.

> To the extent a leader can contain his or her own reactiveness to the reactiveness of followers, principally by focusing on self-functioning rather than changing the functioning of others, intensity tends to wane, and polarization or a cut-off that, like a tango, always takes two, is less likely to be the result....
>
> Leaders have an obligation, to their family (following), to their Creator, and to their species, to keep working at their own self-differentiation.[2]

Some might disagree with Friedman—those who think that leadership is not about headship as much as about helping to get the task done. *Servant leadership* involves empowering the people in the organization.

And in any model, it is important to know who the leader really is: The center is Christ, who is in our "earthen vessels." Followers are to follow us as far as we follow Christ.

Leadership as vision. In *The Seven Habits of Highly Effective People,* Stephen Covey has given a second model of leadership. He has wed a model of psychological maturity with quality management practice and wise practices that are spiritual though not labeled as such. A leader, he says, must have a vision rooted in principles that are greater than the ego of the leader; the vision must help the organization know what it is headed toward. It is not a vision alone: The leader must live from the inside out and demonstrate a character that is organized around principles rather than ego.

> Until individual managers have done the inside-out work, they won't solve the fundamental problems of the organization, nor will they truly empower others, even though they might use the language of empowerment. We must work on character and competence to solve structural and systemic problems.[3]

Spirituality contributes to leadership. The New Testament puts leadership issues in still different language. Timothy is charged to

> Train yourself in godliness; for, while physical training is of some value, godliness is valuable in every way....
> Pay close attention to yourself and to your teaching; continue in these things, for in doing this you will save both yourself and your hearers (1 Tim. 4:7, 16).

This is clearly the equivalent of a differentiated life rooted in principles, not in making people happy.

In Ephesians Paul presents a vision of church unity based upon growing up into Christ, one that can have diversity as people speak the truth in love. How can the church get there? Paul prays for the Ephesians, hoping they will stop being blown about by the opinions of others and find their roots in the deepest reality: that God would

grant that you be strengthened in your inner being with power
through his Spirit, and that Christ may dwell in your hearts through
faith, as you are being rooted and grounded in love. I pray that you
may have the power to comprehend, with all the saints, what is the
breadth and length and height and depth, and to know the love of
Christ that surpasses knowledge, so that you may be filled with all
the fullness of God (Eph. 3:16-19).

So there are several ways to think about leadership, but the best ones
seem to indicate that the leader must change and grow if the organization
is to grow in interdependency, to speak the truth in love, to stop patho-
logical dependencies.

Transformation of Leadership

There are several classic stories of the growth of the soul. One is *The
Divine Comedy,* in which Dante calls the stage of growth "purgatory,"
for there the soul is purged of its sinful character structure. Helen Luke,
a great commentator on Dante's *Divine Comedy,* puts the truth this way:

> As long as we seek to escape from our various "hells" into freedom
> from pain, we remain irremediably bound; we can emerge from the
> pains of Hell by one way only--by accepting another kind of suffer-
> ing, the suffering which is purging, instead of meaningless damna-
> tion.
>   The fire of Purgatory is not a condemnation of desire; Dante
> knows that there is no redemption through cold repression. On the
> contrary it symbolizes the free acceptance of the terrible burning of
> the desire itself endured with the full realization of its redemptive
> meaning; so passing through the fire, the soul finds love.[4]

I don't think that it is a large leap of the imagination to see the fabric
of our lives, our marriages and our jobs, as the place where God has put
us so that we can grow, purged of our self-centeredness.
    In our parish relationships, God calls us to deepen, to struggle not
only for ourselves but for the sake of the others. For my taste *differentiation* is a little tame and scientific to describe this process. So are appeals
for leadership. Even Paul's call that Christ may be in our hearts by faith

omits the battle, the spiritual warfare, the inner and outer cross that is meant to transform us. Transformation is not some self-help idea of deepening the soul for those who have the inclination; it's a life or death struggle—ultimately to lead to world transformation.

I remember my second year in clinical pastoral training in a hospital setting. I thought I had done brilliantly the first summer and would go on to glory in the second year. Instead, I was given a supervisor–in–training who was uptight, angry, and less gifted in many ways than I was. I fought him all summer. At the end of the term, the head chaplain said that he was sorry the summer hadn't worked out well; he had given me to that particular supervisor in the hope that I could be of help to him. Moan. I couldn't see past defending myself. I couldn't see that my problems, seen in the right perspective, could be helpful for others. I don't usually see it even now, but I believe that the purpose of my spiritual warfare is not for my feeling cozy, but to invite God to be at home in my pain and transform me for God's sake and the sake of the people around me.

Transformation is the kind of spiritual power that resided in Bishop Romero, John Wesley, Abraham Lincoln, Julian of Norwich, Fanny Crosby. . . .

And sadly clergy, seminaries, and denominations arrogantly think that clergy can do this by themselves or through some program or another academic degree. But just as Dante needed Virgil, we need help that comes in a variety of ways:

Spiritual formation and guidance. All leaders need spiritual formation and guidance. All clergy need spiritual direction. Spiritual direction has been the single most important contribution to my ministry. I daily see the damage done to congregations by clergy who have no spiritual friend. One of the great insights of Calvin is that sin persists even among the saints, and that we need checks and balances, accountability, the law.

The old desert fathers and mothers insisted on complete transparency before a director. This is the only safe way I know of to be kept from fooling ourselves. It is so easy to have our self-image distorted by the demands of perfection that the profession puts upon us. We need one person who can see us as we are and point us to the call and grace of God. A spiritual director can speak the truth in love.

How do you find a spiritual director? When I first came to Minneapolis as a stranger, I looked up "Jesuit" in the phone book. I eventually wound up with a Cenacle sister trained in Ignatian spiritual direction. These two Roman Catholic orders, Jesuits and Cenacle sisters, specialize in spiritual direction and have high standards of preparation and supervision. The Ignatian system is based on scripture and needs little adjustment for a Protestant directee. Actually, any Roman Catholic order will have spiritual directors. Episcopal priests often know of good directors.

I urge people to shop around. Ask a prospective director about her background and supervision. Generally a director should not be a part of your ecclesiastical system. For younger people, a mentor-director of the same sex is frequently helpful. I have found female directors to be helpful, because there is a natural inclination for men to be competitive with other men. Pastors can benefit from another pastor as director; one's style of leadership can then be open to discernment.

The market is getting flooded with would-be spiritual directors. Many are not the kind of people I would trust to guide my life. Some impose a rigid discipline; others promote one practice only. Some have no supervision, no accountability. Many have no appropriate boundaries to keep the direction relationship safe and distinct. Others have not been trained in psychology and know little about developmental stages and temperaments. Many have not been through long directed retreats and have had no extended opportunity to notice the Spirit's action within.

I have had several different directors. Usually I see my director once a month and delight in being heard. She makes verbal and conscious what I have not fully noticed. Usually I hear something I'd just as soon not hear, but it is ultimately liberating. The heart of the process is my daily examination, and reporting on my journal recordings of what I have perceived God to be doing personally, professionally, and in my marriage.

I also take time off for an annual week-long directed retreat where I try to realign my values and priorities with God's call.

Psychological help. I see a psychologist every month or two for consultation about my professional work. I started seeing him to ensure that I wouldn't get sued in my "private practice." He has been strict in pointing out my limitations, people that I am not trained to help, relationships that require therapy.

He points out when I am expecting "the impossible" of directees because of developmental limitations. He'll ask me, "How old do you think this person is emotionally?" If I say the client is emotionally a teenager, I have a clue about the style of my helping; I have to avoid adolescent power struggles: I do not give material for prayer that can be comprehended only at a later stage of development. I have consistently estimated people to be more developed than he has.

He gives me feedback on my emotional reactions to the people I see. He has been a pastor, is a Protestant, and is my age, so we are really colleagues.

I frequently refer clergy or other church leaders to therapists who deal with addictions, family system problems, and the like. Some estimates indicate that two–thirds of the candidates for ministry come from abusive or dysfunctional families and are in need of therapy.

Help from peers. I also am part of a monthly peer supervision group. Six of us spiritual directors have met together for ten years. We meet monthly for three–and–a–half hours and have an overnight retreat once a year. We pray, relate our life stories, and then do case studies. The issue at hand is not so much "What is wrong with the client or directee or parish?" but, "Where is our distortion?" Why are we defensive or blind or lacking in love, because of the log in our own eye, the sin in our perception? Again and again for ten years, we have seen each others' logs. Now there may be a wry grin as we recognize an "old friend." By talking about it, making it conscious, two things usually happen. First, there is an immediate sense of relief. What was fuzzy or uncomfortable is now clear. Second, as if by magic, the directee frequently changes before we meet together again. Is this some unconscious connection we have? Or is it that we have let go of our blind spot and now can see what God is doing?

I think this group works because we are all professionals; we all take responsibility for leadership. It is also a safe place, where we are not shamed for being vulnerable. In fact, this kind of group helps the healing of shame. We have to work at keeping the sessions from degenerating into gossip or whining or into a review of books and movies with particular spiritual dimensions. We have a regular group inventory and re-align our time and practice.

Help from a peer group led by a facilitator. I am a consultant–facilitator for four clergy groups. One of these had been based on a therapeutic model, looking to heal the clergy of their hang-ups. I have kept this perspective but added a family systems approach and a spiritual direction component. We look at the family of origin of the clergy; how might this unconsciously affect their leadership styles? We usually do a case study that deals with the "outside" and the "inside" of the case. We analyze what is going on "out there" in the parish or with the parishioner but also try to discern what is happening on the inside of the person who presents the case. Where is the call or leading of God here? This is group discernment to pray for insight where God is moving in the parish and in the pastor. In some groups we have a meditation or Bible study.

Individual spiritual direction has a large limitation: It doesn't deal with vocational holiness, helping the pastor or leader discern the Spirit of God in the congregation. Vocational spirituality or the discernment of the Holy Spirit's activity in a parish or group is best facilitated in groups and among people with whom we feel safe to admit our need for help. This kind of group, with a case study discipline wedded with contemplative prayer, works well to help the participants look at the call of God out there in the parish, and in here, in us. As Paul says: "Test yourselves.... You need firsthand evidence, not mere heresay, that Jesus Christ is in you" (2 Cor. 13:5 TM).

Help from lay groups or "spiritual friends." Both Befriender and Stephen Ministry lay trainees meet regularly in groups. These frequently move into spiritual direction issues. Much of this book has been written with these lay ministers in mind. In my parish I meet with leaders of small groups to support them and help them plan.

For six years I've belonged to a men's group—friends outside the parish who meet for breakfast to talk about work, wives, children, and coping. Sometimes I think we could all be taken inside a sweat lodge or kiva where more primitive men did the same sort of thing. Sometimes I think words are not necessary—grunts, chants, and perhaps silence speak volumes. Men especially need groups where they can reclaim their power and ability to help one another. Women seem to know this naturally, or at least more easily than men.

Also, another male spiritual director and I meet once a month as spiritual friends. The framework of this relationship is different from spiritual direction, or we come at it differently. I listen to him for half an hour, and he does the same for me. There is *mutual* vulnerability and *mutual* accountability. And we continually articulate where we see the other hiding and resisting God's call to freedom and love. We talk about the daily leadings in our marriages, in our professions, and in our direct relationship with God. I have tried this with several people and it has not been productive. Why, with him? I don't know.

Images of Vocational Identity

When we start living from the inside out, when we start responding to the Holy Spirit instead of to the spirit of the world, we may want to rethink our pastoral identity. I'm afraid that as young pastors, we spend a lot of time trying to figure it out intellectually, when in actuality we learn by being and doing. And what we usually learn by doing is that parishioners pay us to run the church, preach sermons, and call on the sick. They want religion, American style. God calls us to piety or spirituality or sanctification.

Whether we see ourselves as pastors, priests, preachers, or pastoral-managers, those roles can be just the opposite of what God has intended. We might use new names—"contemplative pastor," "spiritual director," or "spiritual guide"—but applying a new label won't change us. But I recently came upon a phrase that put into words what I have been feeling: "We are guides into God's most sublime secrets, not security guards posted to protect them (1 Cor. 4:2 TM). Guides into God's most sublime secrets: Christ in us, the hope of glory. *That* is what I believe we are supposed to be doing.

I strongly encourage leaders to write down a mission statement and refer to it often (see chapter 7). The road to hell is paved with good intentions. I know I need to remind myself of my priorities.

And to do that I know that I need help and structures to keep me on target, to help me respond to the leading of the Spirit. Follow the example of Jesus, who invited three disciples to join him in the Garden of Gethsemane. He was lonely. And Paul—in prison he wrote asking Timothy to "Come before winter" (2 Tim. 4:21).

Ask for help and friends in the garden or before winter comes. Invite a friend or a group to be with you. In such a manner God has transformed people before you.

CHAPTER 10

Adult Stages of Development

To be spiritually alive means to be growing and changing . . .
A saint is simply a human being whose soul has thus
grown up to its full stature.[1]

So says Evelyn Underhill, the towering writer of spirituality classics, in a lecture for clergy. I learned about development and growth from another source.

My wife and I started parenting with a book at hand. When we didn't know what to do with our baby, we opened the book and read about the problem. Frequently we found help or discovered that it was time to call the doctor. As time passed, when our child's behavior was unusual, we'd again open the book. It often said she was going through a developmental stage. This knowledge was a comfort. It also meant that we could cooperate with God's timing instead of working against it.

There are patterns of development in children and adults where some things have to happen before others can. Parents can't force an "inner readiness" for a developmental stage. Research of the French psychologist Piaget showed, for instance, that children were ready to read at a certain stage of brain formation. Styles of thinking also progress as a child matures. Early infants have magical thinking. Older children develop cause–and–effect thinking, and much later, abstract thinking. But consider the fact that the capacity for abstract thinking is missing from at least half of the adults in America. This understanding of development has profound implication for sermons, spiritual growth, and living in community.

As there are stages of physical development, theorists also see stages of adult moral development. Until the 1980s most of the research and thought has been done by men. Carol Gilligan showed how men's presuppositions skewed theories of moral and spiritual development. Robert Kegan, Harvard psychologist and colleague of Carol Gilligan, has constructed a theory that is inclusive of male and female points of view. His theory is very important for understanding spirituality, for his system deals with how we construct meaning. The great French spiritual director Jean-Pierre de Caussade says that spirituality is the proper "way of viewing things." Depending on our stage of psychological development, we may be quite limited in how much we can grow in our "way of viewing things" from God's perspective. And those who are helping to form the souls of others must know about the limitations of various stages of psychological development. The stages of psychological growth affect moral and spiritual development.

To put this another way, the Myers–Briggs Type Indicator (MBTI) provides a pattern of thinking about the differences among personalities. Wise pastors and leaders have always understood that people are different. The MBTI makes these patterns explicit, largely along a horizontal plane. There is another way to account for differences on a wholly different dimension. I think of the MBTI as the horizontal, the stages of adult development as the vertical. Why do we need this augmenting? The MBTI as it is usually taught gives no clues for growth. It seems to identify a point of view that justifies our remaining one-sided. Adult development theory offers a guide to growth in another dimension: Adult development theory is important both to show people how their spiritual lives might grow and to help leaders learn how others are different from themselves. Why do leaders need this? It is extremely common for pastors or teachers or leaders of a small group to assume that everyone else in the group is pretty much like them.

This is a mistaken assumption and may do great harm to others. Take, for instance, the common description of spirituality as "the inner life." Most of the adults in church on a Sunday morning are incapable of having an inner life in terms of being able to sort out different feelings and thoughts. Their psychological development doesn't offer a framework for this. For most people the "inner life" is chaotic, random, and stereotyped. Most people can't stand much silence, many can't visualize in meditation, and yet leaders regularly inflict these practices on parishioners or spiritual directors on directees. Then the parishioners give up and feel depressed or grow angry with their pastor.

Unfortunately the theory of psychological development cannot be learned to put into practice simply from books or lectures. It is an abstract way of thinking about humans and in my experience takes a long time to put into practice. I have learned it from a psychologist who teaches it to spiritual directors and therapists. I am supervised once a month, and it took more than two years before most of my clinical judgments about people coincided with his. Even now I tend to overestimate where people are, particularly if they are smart, well-educated professionals.

But by reading this brief chapter, you can learn that people must be treated with great respect, that you must not foist off on others the practices you find nourishing, and that you need to pay attention to where the other person is—more important, pay attention to where God is working in the other person.

Psychological development and spiritual maturity or holiness are not the same thing. A child can be holy, and Therese of Liseux was a saint at age twenty–four. But one's psychological stage of development sets the frame, provides the setting for the spirit. We may think of one's psychological stage of development as the jar that is the container for the liquid, the spirit—or as the cookie cutter that makes the shape for the person's life. (We also identified the MBTI as a container for the spirit; again, the two categorizations are complementary, like horizontal and vertical dimensions of a life.)

The following material is based on the ideas of Robert Kegan.[2] The words describing the stages and the relationships are those of Sam Keen.[3]

Stages of Psychological Growth and Spiritual Implications

Stages	Attributes	Relationships
1. child	basic trust openness, wonder curiosity magical thinking	dependent
2. rebel	new peer group romance doubt, blame others antagonistic literal thinking	counterdependent
3. young adult	membership vows duty, sense of belonging sacrifice for future law-and-order thinking	mutually dependent
3–1/2. transition	inner authority fragile and developing self-awareness probing commitment	fragile self-dependent
4. adult	independent self-acceptance owning own darkness reconciling opposites	confident self- or inner-dependent
5. wise adult	unitive glimpse love of all radical trust God in all things	interdependent

This looks so simple and self-explanatory; how could it be difficult to incorporate this into our thinking? First of all, it is abstract and not easily incorporated into our experience. (I will suggest some movies and themes that may help identify characteristics of each stage.) Second, recognizing patterns in real-life people takes patience and practice and clinical or practical help from a supervisor or group.

Insights into Stages

Stage 1. We are all familiar with the childlike way of perceiving God in stories and in magical thinking. Many books help identify the various subdivisions in children's thinking. We all may revert to this stage in crisis, and when we are victimized we often stay here for a while. Many of the mentally ill live in this stage.

Stage 2. Adolescents or stage-2 rebels are not independent but counterdependent. They need adults and a tradition to rebel against; that is how they make meaning. Those raising adolescents yearn for them to get through this stage, yet there is a delightful quality of stage–2 people. This is often seen in men who have made a lot of money. They are like the hero in Tom Hanks's movie *Big*. In the movie a boy gets a man's body and does very well in the toy-designing business. Because he thinks like a boy, he knows instinctively what a boy would like.

Some stage-2 single men may admit the reason they pick up women isn't so much for the sex as for the company, having a friend in the house. Perhaps for many men, sexual conquest and making money is basically an adolescent dream that masks the even deeper longings of childhood. People who are perpetual adolescents are most likely stuck in chronic resentment, passive dependency, incurable romanticism, and/or the playboy or playgirl game.

The transition from stage 2 to 3 is seen in AA. The Twelve Steps work on responsibility for oneself being aligned with a higher power. Traditional conversions occur here.

Stage 3. Stage 3 is where you could classify most of the leadership in most churches and denominations. These people are mutually dependent on others for their identity. Their inner life is not developed, making them very vulnerable to what others think and say. Their "external" religion is easily threatened by the opposition, and they tend to "dig in," defensively telling people what to do and believe. I found stage–3 thinking in a "liberal" seminary that would not allow Billy Graham to come and speak. There was a closed mind about conservatives. In stage–3 thinking, the like-minded close ranks; this is splitting many denominations.

Stage 3–1/2. This is seen as a stage of its own, calling forth great resources for change. In Henrik Ibsen's *A Doll's House,* the wife, Nora, is a childish stage 1 or 2. She can't handle money and is charmingly irresponsible. Her very responsible, banker, respectable–stage–3 husband delights in being paternalistic. Through much suffering Nora becomes a stage 3-1/2. When her husband finds that she has made decisions about money behind his back, he is furious. She decides to leave him, seeing that he is wrongly enraged at her for spending the money—on him, on his recovery from illness. The husband feels justified digging in his heels; the church and the law say that wives are supposed to stay with their husbands.

Nora isn't so sure about "what is right"; she will have to dig into her own experience to find that out. The husband doesn't get it. If he is like a lot of men, he will find another sweet young thing to take care of until she, too, matures. And that woman may also eventually leave to find her soul, just as the prodigal son had to leave for the far country.

A men's scenario of a stage-3-1/2 transition is evident in the movie comedy *City Slickers.* Three men in their midlife crisis go to a dude ranch where they meet up with a tough foreman. The boss says, "You have to find out what number one is—you have to find it out by yourself." After a harrowing experience herding cattle, each finds out what they care about more than making money or having fun. The men are changed from being rather shallow and stereotypical to being centered and focused.

Sometimes this transition happens in college, more often in midlife. But for the majority, never. It is always hard to grow beyond the group norm. The norm for most churches is conformity, and for this reason small groups that seek spiritual growth often are perceived to be threatening the perspective of the majority. During this transition the person particularly needs a group or spiritual director to support the growth to which God may be calling.

Stage 4. Stage 4 is usually reached only after much help through mentoring. Stage-4 people have ceased to blame others for their problems and avoid shaming themselves. They can understand sin as the darkness within them and can take responsibility for themselves. They are capable of true discernment, classically understood as sorting out where God is in the thoughts and feelings inside. (People in stages 3 and 3–1/2 may be able to notice their feelings but are not usually able to detach from them.)

Up through stage 3, people equate God's will with learning from principles, rules. "Forget your feelings. Do what is right," said one of my early guides. But those of us who are growing need to notice our feelings, because finally we can discern God's call in the feelings, thoughts, and motions of the Spirit within. The master spiritual director, Ignatius of Loyola, gave interesting rules for discernment. For beginners, it is following the rules and principles given by the church. For the more advanced, it is paying attention to the inner movements of the Holy Spirit. For the most mature, it is sorting through these and seeing which ones lead to God and which ones are destructive.

What helps people move through transitions? The twelve steps of AA are set up to help people move from stage 2 to 3. You have to accept a higher power than your own rebelliousness and begin some spiritual disciplines. Stephen Covey's *The Seven Habits of Highly Effective People* is useful for consolidating and moving to stage 4. The book is founded on adult developmental theory.

Sometimes a whole community will show evidence of being in stage 5. *Weapons of the Spirit,* a documentary repeated on PBS, is the story of a small village in France that hid five thousand Jews during World War II. Most of the hosts belonged to a French Huguenot church that had good leadership and a heritage of its own suffering. When asked to shelter refugees, the townspeople did immediately, not because they were told to or because everyone was doing it, but because it was the right thing to do. As these people were interviewed on television, they seemed solid, really there. There was no strain; they were who they were. They were differentiated and in community, practicing truly ethical behavior and in touch with God, others, and their true selves.

Gender Differences and Developmental Theory

Just as church leaders should be aware of differences in temperament and in developmental stages, we should be aware of gender–based differences. We also need to know that even "enlightened" literature can stereotype men and women in ways that are not universally applicable.

In terms of developmental theory, the following chart gives some insight into how men and women in various stages might differ in relation to (1) a specific developmental task and (2) a growing edge— what someone at this stage "needs" to "move on."

Male–Female Development

STAGE	2	3	3 1/2	4
General task	being accountable	meeting group expectations	finding personal authority	being at home with oneself or others
General need	being in relationship	finding values inside	operating from "who I am"	seeing universal heros and heroines
Men's patterns	being delusionally dominant	being paternalistically masculine	taking risks, being direct	moving toward wise man
Men's need	not being abusive, being responsible for their own behavior	being in touch with anger at male stereotypes	reaching out, no longer blaming women	being oneself in relationship
Women's patterns	being delusionally subordinate	being maternalistically feminine	assertively taking risks	moving toward wise woman
Women's need	not being victims, saying no	getting in touch with anger at stereotypes	deciding no longer to to blame men, working on selves	being oneself in relationship

See the bibliography for more information on gender differences.
As you work in church groups, know that God has made us—male and
female—in the image of God. Generally, a pastor and group leaders
need extra help to interpret the experiences of the opposite gender. The
best training is with a mixed group—men and women who are past stereotyped responses. Consider also the following implications for differences in gender.

Need for language and examples that fit both genders. Encourage
the use of inclusive language, so that both men and women feel their
needs are addressed. Women may have different images of God than
men. Men may see their besetting sin as arrogance. Men may be stuck
at the stages of rebellion or autonomy. We want to fight being dependent. In actuality, men may be quite dependent—on the women in their
lives. A marriage may look like a big daddy and a little girl or helper,
but actually it might be a big mom and a little boy who is being taken
care of.

Women, on the other hand, may find that their besetting sin is being
too dependent. But the secret reality? They are often quite capable of
living without men. On "happiness" polls, single women score higher
than married women (while single men score lower than married men).

When men or women move from one stage to another and internal-
ize new roles—or when inclusive language is introduced in the liturgy—
expect resistance, even hostility.

Some different groups for men and for women. At some point most
men need male support groups and women need women's groups to
make the transition into maturity. As a rule, in a group setting men are
more reluctant to talk about their souls than women. I've had more luck
talking to the younger men in my parish on a one-to-one basis than in
groups.

Another pattern is often a matter of the "right timing": At times a
mature man can provide a woman a chance to reparent herself, and at
times a man can best be helped by a woman.

In terms of women's groups, traditional groups often do not meet the
need of younger women, who often find it easier to share their struggles,
for instance of balancing marriage and work. On the other hand, many
older women often just don't see why the younger ones aren't as willing
as they to engage in church volunteer work.

There are books that describe these shifts in other words. Betty
Friedan talks about men moving from macho to being in touch with their

feelings, and then still deeper, being more fully men. She has suggested that liberated women may over-do their toughness and that it may be more useful to move to a deeper phase of being women.

Mentoring Leaders

As I lead support groups for clergy, I find that leaders below stage 4 are so dependent upon the good will of the congregation (or group) that they become defensive whenever anyone suggests they are less than perfect. Clergy and leaders at a lower stage of development have their reference point in being popular or ideas about church that come from the culture, not a center that is rooted and grounded in God. In seminary or in the ongoing support given by denominations, clergy and laity are usually not helped in deepening and maturing. In my experience there may be some growth in intellectual content in seminary, but the ability to relate to God and others is usually less mature after seminary than before.

When I am training laity to lead small groups, I look for those who have developed their inner life, moving into stage 3–1/2, perhaps through counseling or spiritual direction. I try to help them sort out the differences between those who need rules and those who can be encouraged to ask God directly and find the answers within. If leaders are able to listen to others and reflect back what they hear, they are usually saved from giving bad advice. If they can discern where God might be calling the other and ask a question about this, that's even better. If they can refer the other person to God, encourage that person to ask what God is saying, doing, being—that is the most effective method I know.

Typical Congregations

The fact remains that most of the people in congregations I have served are at stage 2 or 3. Stage–2 people can be good at making money, and they prefer rather simple approaches in church. Instead of looking down my nose at this, I may appreciate their generosity expressed in a different way than mine. Earlier I would have assumed that my theological or spiritual taste was better than theirs and that my duty was to educate them. Now I think that we are simply at different stages, and it is my job to speak to them where they are.

If that is so, how can we preach to or teach a group of people at

various stages? Again, we need to start where people are. To get a sense
of a group, I may ask a few leading questions if I am dealing with special
material. I'll start with stories that may involve all. Then I'll express the
idea in simple language. After a while I may shift gears, as I sense some
dropping out and others showing more interest. I think of a black preacher who, in the sixties, said, he had to use the word *colored* for the older
folks, *negro* for the less militant, and *black* for the young and the militant.

Here's how it might look to preach inclusively to a group that includes people at stages 2, 3, and 4. Let's consider the topic of suffering.

At stage 2 people understand that "Life isn't fair." Accepting the
Buddhist idea that life is suffering is a mighty achievement for this stage.
The AA material works well for this stage.

Stage–3 people may see and accept one reason we suffer: because
we love people. Children's books such as *The Little Prince* and *The
Velveteen Rabbit* give messages like this at several levels.

Folks in stage 3–1/2 may understand suffering as the price we pay
for being human and individual. We find who we are in the midst of
pain; we discover our voice in the midst of conflict. At this stage the
Garden of Eden may represent the tragic necessity for leaving father and
mother, leaving childhood, leaving what society thinks. Sharing that
pain with another may be quite possible in nonstereotypical ways. Instead of feeling like a victim, the person may identify with the sufferings
of Jesus in a healthy way.

People in stage 4 may see our hearts being purified in conflict and in
suffering; they may see the crucifixion as an inner experience of one's
ego putting to death one's true self or Christ within. We are no longer
innocents; we actually put Christ to death. This is outside and historical,
and inside and spiritual. To put this another way, our egos continually
put the image of God in us to death. We have met the enemy and the
enemy is us. The spiritual writings about purification make sense in
stage 4.

My guess is that stage–5 people are so individuated that they find
God in all things, including their suffering, and probably don't need
sermons to help. They may listen to the same stories heard by people in
other stages, but they will universalize them.

Exercise

Imagine that you are trying to present the idea that God is love; you will include examples based on experience. Refer to the "stages" chart given in this chapter. How will "God is love" be translated into experience at each of the six stages?

For the next group or sermon, see if you can intentionally speak to people in stages 2, 3, and 3–1/2.

Talk this over with someone who understands it and practice guessing where people are and inviting the expert opinion.

CHAPTER 11

Development and Spiritual Growth

Evelyn Underhill and her Roman Catholic spiritual director, Baron von Hugel, both recognized patterns in differences among people. They also understood that people and congregations and denominations changed and grew. Evelyn spoke to pastors:

> You will never be able to make another soul see reality from exactly the same spiritual angle as yourself.[1]

> The obstinate pursuit of a special state of meditation or recollection always defeats itself. . . . The important thing is to discover what nourishes you, best expands and harmonizes your spirit, now, *at the present stage of your growth.*[2]

Pastors and lay leaders will make mistakes. Perhaps the most frequent is assuming that another person or the group will respond to the same thing the same way that we do. Sometimes that does happen—if what we present is sufficiently universal or profound. But many times it doesn't work.

I remember first arriving to serve at a large church. I had just finished my master's degree in spirituality; for four summers I had spent intensive periods of time meditating daily with a student group. I felt the method we used, contemplative meditation, was *the* way, although I wouldn't have said that. In the new parish I introduced myself to the major group of leaders by leading a meditation prayer: in silence focusing on breathing; visualizing a biblical story and carrying on a dialogue with Jesus. People went through the motions and said nothing in response. But at the next staff meeting, it was strongly suggested that I stick with verbal prayer.

I have since learned two important lessons: People need lots of preparation, and people are different—by temperament and in their stages of development.

I have seen lay leaders come back from Cursillo meetings and want to reshape the congregation around that activity. Others have gone off to journaling workshops or weekends for centering prayer and have become evangelists for this new method. Some insist that Sophia should be on the lips of everyone or that men should drum with Robert Bly. They learn painfully that most people are not interested, and that doubling their zeal only makes them fanatical or depressed. God is trying to teach us to be humble and to respect differences.

My advice about spiritual growth, my preaching and administration, and my training of group leaders has all been radically changed because of my knowledge of adult development.

We don't expect a one–year–old to read books. Yet I have given spiritual exercises, such as practicing the presence of God, and assumed that participants could do it if they tried hard enough. Wrong! I have made mistakes again and again when I assumed that my parishioners saw the reality of the parish the same way I did, and that *my way was right.* Again and again I hear clergy or lay leaders hurt or angry because people haven't responded to their leadership in the way they had expected. When I ask for details, it is obvious that the parishioners' responses are quite understandable and predictable.

I see differences along two axes: the horizontal axis being the temperament differences seen through the MBTI, the vertical axis being the developmental difference. This provides two coordinates for sorting out where people might be coming from.

Some know these differences intuitively. Evelyn Underhill talked about three types of approaches to prayer and the necessity of the pastor treating everyone uniquely. Most classical spiritual guides talk about different "weeks" (Ignatius) or stages such as beginners, intermediates, and proficients (many authors).

Dangers in Applying Developmental Theory

Yet I see at least three significant dangers to the application of adult developmental theory.

First, our achievement orientation encourages us to rank people according to their development; we will try to help people make it to the next stage whether or not God is calling that way, whether or not the people want to change. Even worse, we may think that we need to grow ourselves to be at the stage above us; we may want to make our spiritual life an achievement. This is so obviously ego–centered it hardly seems worth noting. Growth is a gift. "Which of you by taking thought can add one cubit unto his stature?" asked Jesus (Matt. 6:27 KJV).

The second danger: Once we label, we think that we know. We do know some things, such as the direction of a compass. We can memorize scripture and know some of the symptoms of mental illness. We do not know how God is uniquely dealing with a particular person. Distinguishing between what we know as a pattern and what we know as we hear the inner thoughts and feelings of a person takes some skill. One kind of knowledge is the knowledge of patterns or diagnosis. The other is the reflective knowledge from the Spirit or discernment. Supervision can help us practically address the two kinds of knowledge. Working with a person, I usually move back and forth between the two kinds of knowledge. I may start off with the developmental classification so that I have a rough idea of what park we are playing in. Then I forget this, or lay it aside, and just listen. I listen with my mind and with my heart and with my imagination. After the person has left, I think it all over and try to put the pieces together and pray for the person.

The third danger from stage theory is that we may take the lowest common denominator and think that psychological maturity is the same as holiness. It is not, and yet many times there is a relationship between maturity and sanctification. Many people fall into this trap of confusing psychology with spiritual growth. I have trouble seeing this material in terms of "faith development." Faith as trust is *in God*. Faith development focuses on our thinking about God. We need to know where people are developmentally, but the focus is on God, in the person's perception of God.

To go back to the two axes of temperamental and developmental differences, I think that holiness or our spirituality is a circle reaching out from the intersection of the two lines. This forms a Celtic cross!

Despite these dangers and warnings, adult developmental theory provides a helpful system, a framework, for noticing maturational differences: helpful for parish and one–on–one spiritual guidance and insightful for determining where the growing edge might be for individual members and the whole parish. I see more mistakes made because of ignorance of stages and patterns than of the theory's misuse.

In the chart on page 113, I give an outline of changing patterns for helping people as they move from one stage to another. For each stage I give a rough suggestion of what spiritual practices might be appropriate. This is based on established theory and also from feedback from my parish and my directees.

Hints for Spiritual Practices

Stages	2	3	3 1/2	4
Hints				
support needed	group	leader group mutuality	mentor peers	individual self-selected group
growing edge	accountability ego not God	Higher Power God in us Covenant	God in me God in us	God the center
role of guide	friend	guide teacher	mentor classical spiritual director	mutual
inventory or examination of consciousness	look for wrongs, promptly admit	look at relationships	look at the movement of the Spirit inside	moment-by-moment discerning
meditation	thinking about principles	savor the truth	silence images	presence
prayer	your will	my deepest longing	contemplation being with	prayed through

Here is a more detailed explanation of the terms:

Support: When we make significant changes in our inner life, we usually need support. People in stage 2 need to be part of a gang, a supportive group. Most often the group is informal, centered around some activity; the group is often "against" something or someone else. Support becomes more formal in stage 3, where the gang becomes the choir, the clergy association, or the Al-Anon group. Some people never get beyond the stage–3 identity that comes from being a Harvard graduate or from wearing a clerical collar or from being the wife of a doctor. Eventually some want to be part of a smaller group dealing with more interesting and personal issues. These peer groups encourage further individuation more than role and doing it right. The people at stage 3-1/2 may also want to find a guide to talk to. In stage 4 people hand–select a group they want to be with for their own unique purposes.

Growing edge: When people are secure and grounded enough to move, they entertain the idea of change, growth, deepening. For stage 2, growth involves realizing that my own ego is not God, nor is the group's ego. There is a Higher Power. We mortals are limited, powerless in some areas. This becomes a more deeply held realization for stage 3. Additionally, stage–3 people realize that God is not only above but in relationships. God is in the group, in the Ten Commandments, in the Bible, and we are able to make a decision to commit ourselves to God, to marriage, to church, to a spiritual discipline. Later this deepens, and God is in me. I am able to look at my experience and know the call of God. Finally I come to a deeper surrender, and God is the center of my life; I find God in everything (stage 5).

Role of guide: The nature of the helper moves from being a buddy or friend in stage 2 through mutual accountability to being a mentor, to finally being a true spiritual director in the classical sense. In practical terms this means that adolescents need a friend, a companion; many who come for help are still at this stage and will mightily resist any direct use of authority for boundaries or limits. Obviously parents and leaders need to set limits anyway, but leaders must use care with rebellious folks. The less reactive or angry the leader, the easier it is for everyone. People in stage 3 want the leaders to be leaders, though some class differences might be evident here. Blue–collar workers expect the boss to be the boss. Young, managerial types may want a more collaborative style. People at this stage expect leadership in direction, and I usually give printed material detailing what patterns of inventory, prayer, or meditation the person might find useful.

Classical spiritual direction cannot begin until people are in stage 3–1/2. When I started spiritual direction, I struggled to get the "right" answer rather than facing my inner life. I remember running away from the silence because I couldn't stand it. One director responded by giving me books to read. The one who was more helpful said, "Do the examen. What is God saying in your life?" Another suggested that I give up books on spirituality for Lent. The most helpful director asked me what God was like as I prayed. This director encouraged me to speak my heart to God. It is a gift to know when to go with the directee's flow, when to work with the growing edge, and when to suggest new methods, new exercises.

What does this "role of guide" category say to pastors? Most people in most congregations are in stages 2 or 3. Despite their level of education, most will be needing a pastor to be a friend or a teacher. When you preach, start at stage 2 and work up. Telling stories works for most stages. Those who want to get into small groups for spiritual growth will more than likely be in stage 3–1/2. If they stay in small groups with like-minded folks, the self-enclosed enclaves may be alienated from the rest of the congregation. I suggest that groups re–form each year. These folks can act as leaven for the whole congregation!

And what does this "role of guide" category say to group leaders? Putting together a group with stage–3 people is tricky. Threes are likely to be scared by the way stage 3–1/2–people talk. We usually are threatened by people more developed than we are. The trick or art is to affirm the less developed, explaining and showing that we are where we should be, while at the same time letting the more advanced share their experience as a model.

Inventory: The last three categories on the chart are three patterns of classical practice as identified in the twelve steps of Alcoholics Anonymous: inventory (or examen), prayer, and meditation.

An inventory of personal liabilities cuts through denial of unhealthy behavior. Looking at positive things is good too. This basic inventory is achievable in stage 2. Those in stage 3 can look at more subtle things: their relationship with God, with significant people. They may be able to look at a mission statement and measure their behavior against it.

At stage 3-1/2 people can begin to look inward and ask where the prompting of the Holy Spirit is. They may be able to detach from some of their immediate reactions. I can distinctly remember the first time I consciously did this. At a costume party my wife and I arrived dressed in street clothes. I was mortified because I'd missed the note on the invitation about costumes. As a whole the group was terribly careful about clothes and propriety. But I checked out my feelings, and I said, *I can choose to act like a jerk all evening, or I can forget my mistake and have some fun.* I decided to have fun.

At stage 4 we check out subtle movements, paying attention to our own bodies, listening to critics; we are quite able to carry on an inner dialogue with God. We are able to understand parts of scripture that formerly puzzled us. We are able to find the presence or absence of God in all things fairly quickly and simply. When we can't, we're able to ask for help.

Meditation. Meditation (AA step 11) is usually understood at stage 2 as listening to God. And this usually comes from reading a daily devotional lesson, remembering the thought for today, and moving on.

For those in stage 3, meditation may continue with the same pattern or become more active in thinking about God, even thinking with God. At this stage it seems important to get orthodox answers, whatever passes for orthodox in a particular group.

At stage 3–1/2 there is a shift. Here the MBTI thinking types may need special help to move to contemplation, "looking at" with wonder. Feeling types may begin the transition by paying attention to their hearts being "strangely warmed." They may learn to think about the truth that is different from their heart feeling. Thinking types may move past skeptical thinking to relish the truth. If questioned closely, they may say they mull over their daily reading all day. All types may write sayings in a notebook or motion to their hearts and say, "That really got to me." Here we see the possibility for more inward meditation, for visualization, contemplation, centering prayer, breath prayer. Silence can be tolerated and even enjoyed.

Somewhere later comes the ability to find God in all things, to practice the presence of God throughout the day, to know divine union.

Prayer. The prayer of surrender is not the only prayer used in Alcoholics Anonymous any more than it is the only prayer in the Bible. But it points to the most profound truth of our prayer life: "thy will be done." Praying helps us discover what that will is.

Stage–2 prayer at best may be a conversation with God, my friend Jesus, my "Higher Power." The content is largely praying for things and for miraculous interventions. There may be a surrender, but it is partial, more like compliance.

At stage 3 prayer is often more stereotyped, with a long list of concerns for doing it "right." I kept trying to get the right book for me, not aware that *I* needed to change, not the book. At the end of C. S. Lewis's *Till We Have Faces,* the heroine says, "I saw well why the gods do not speak to us plainly, nor let us answer. Till that word can be dug out of us, why should they hear the babble that we think we mean? How can they meet us face to face until we have faces?"

We don't have faces until we notice the shadowlands inside us. As long as we still see evil and sin only on the outside, as long as we keep blaming someone else and remain victims, we will have trouble seeing God face to face or knowing Christ within. Until we see ourselves as we are in the light of God, we cannot know God fully.

That begins to be possible at stage 3–1/2 and is not complete until stage 4 and beyond. As we become more vulnerable, more transparent, our psychological defenses become lower, and we have increasing opportunities for intimacy.

Talk versus Practice

People can talk the language of a particular stage before they are able to practice it. And a lot of people are ready for more intimacy with God, but because of their family systems and/or lack of encouragement, they fail to go where God is calling. Yet grace is surprising and persistent and saints come from unlikely congregations. Despite our lacks and resistance, God does wonderful things to contradict and delight us.

Theresa of Avila suffered under terrible spiritual directors for years. Her directors, pious people though they were, thought they knew how she should be praying. They were dead wrong. Theresa recognized that knowledge, experience, and discernment—along with piety—was very important in a spiritual guide. I agree. And much of that knowledge can come as we learn the patterns of psychological development and their spiritual implications.

PART THREE

Putting This into Practice

CHAPTER 12

Spiritual Support for the Laity

An Annual Spiritual Checkup

I'm ashamed to admit that I'm just learning how to give parish leaders an annual spiritual checkup. Oh, I called on people before. In my first parish, I learned to ask "How's the old problem doing?" People would talk on forever about their spouses, gall bladders, the communist conspiracy, or whatever.

That tack for personalized ministry led to others, but I eventually came upon the old pastoral model as described in The Reformed Pastor by Richard Baxter. Baxter lived in the 1600s and established the practice of having his parishioners visit him once a year. At that time he inquired into their faith, spirituality, and relationships. I had long wished that I could do that but lacked the courage.

After our governing body discovered its mission, we wondered how we could find out if we were helping people in their relationship with God, others, and themselves. Together we decided that if we thought that spirituality was important, we should ask people about their spiritual life. It sounds pretty logical but seemed quite revolutionary at the time.

I designed a questionnaire with the help of some parishioners, tried it out on the congregation, and had no violent resistance. Some appreciated the questions, others just used a simple checklist (see "Spiritual Life Questions for a Congregation" at the end of this chapter).

I asked the congregation as a whole to look at the questionnaire, so the leaders would know the kind of questions I might ask in a private interview. I now use the questionnaire at least yearly, often in an attempt to motivate people to look at themselves.

Then I asked three of the most receptive church leaders if they would be willing to talk with me privately in my office about their spiritual life. They were a little doubtful, but they knew me and thought it probably wouldn't be too weird.

These three pioneers enjoyed the interviews. I asked them to stand up in church and describe the interview experience, to encourage others. Then I called on the rest of the church leaders.

I would start the interview by asking how the person felt about this session. I then explained how I intended to proceed. I'd ask something rather safe, such as, "How is it going with you?" Listening to the answer, I'd go on to something like, "And how goes your spiritual life?" I would ask about his relationship with God and others, work, and self-esteem.

Sometimes I'd say, "If life were college, what would the name be of the course you're in?" If they didn't get that, I'd ask, "Where is the growing edge of your life? Where is God leading or nudging?" Sometimes I asked about priorities. Then I'd work with them to devise some sort of a program or support so they might move.

For instance, many of the people I called on last summer said that they wanted to be more aware of God during the day. So last fall we designed a program with an emphasis on practicing the presence of God.

Winding things up, I'd ask how they liked the interview, what was uncomfortable; was there anything else they'd like to say?

As a result of these interviews, I have a much better idea of where the leaders are and what is important to them. It makes preaching a lot easier. I feel close to them, and I am confident that we are developing a climate of openness in the church. Some wanted to follow up for a few sessions, and we did. I asked participants who expressed high interest to be leaders of small groups this year. My belief is that leading spiritual groups is a matter of spiritual and psychological maturity. I can teach techniques, but I can't produce mature leaders. What I can do is notice what God is doing in the lives of my leaders, see where there is growth, and hope others will "catch" the maturity.

I continue the dialogue with many, offering assurance. Some tell me when prayer gets hard or stops. Some ask for a book.

As in formal spiritual direction, I often take some notes and pray afterwards. I don't see this as a formal spiritual direction relationship but more what I have called spiritual guidance. (Even in an informal spiritual guidance relationship with parishioners, we need to make a relational shift when we meet to work together or worship together. I am quite able to make this shift, but in a more formal relationship it is usually more complicated.)

These leadership calls have affected my ordinary pastoral calls. I find I inwardly ask the question "Where is God in this person's life?" What I say and how I pray will be informed by what I perceive the spiritual reality to be. The same is true with church meetings. Sometimes I openly ask, "What has God been doing in our midst?" Other times, I just share what I discern and ask others to comment.

It is said that the English town in which Richard Baxter pastored showed signs of his ministry more than a hundred years after he left. There was a real religious awakening and deepening that changed lives and the community. May it happen today!

Training Lay Spirituality–Group Leaders

Leaders of spiritual growth groups need to be growing in their own spiritual lives. They probably need to be in the transitional stage 3–1/2. It is more important for them to model openness than to know facts about God, spirituality, or the Bible. Before leading others, they need to be thoroughly grounded in their own path. This means that they have been through the Beginning Again material and have sustained some practice of spiritual awareness.

For training, I schedule a minimum of six or eight weekly sessions, two hours a session. I supplement this by weekly leadership–support meetings once they are leading groups.

I work with the following training themes, presented here in order of priority:

1. Focus on spirituality. What are we aiming for, and what kind of help are we offering?
2. How a spiritual growth group works.
3. Ways of leading meditative prayer and encouraging experiential learning.
4. How to encourage another. How not to do harm.
5. Stages in adult growth.
6. Myers-Briggs Type Indicator—temperaments and application.

Spiritual Life Questions for a Congregation

"Examine yourself, do you not know that God is in you?" That's what the apostle Paul encouraged. So we ask you to examine yourself.

Part 1

1. How would you describe your spiritual life at the present?

2. How would you describe your relationship with God. Why do you give this answer? What about your relationship with others? Can you cherish your strengths and your weaknesses?

3. What is the growing edge in your life; that is, where is God leading your to grow?

4. In which area of life would you like some spiritual help?

Part 2

This may be difficult. Jesus summarized God's will for us: "You shall love the Lord your God with all your heart, and with all your soul, and with all your mind, and with all your strength. Your shall love your neighbor as yourself." (Mark 12: 30-31) He also assumed we would have some kind of spiritual practice: To introduce the "Lord's Prayer," he said "when you pray. . . " not "If you pray . . ."

Please respond by circling one number along a continuum, realizing that your resonse would vary from day to day.

Not at all	**Some**	**Mostly**

My relationship with God:

1. I am growing in my awareness of and love for God, in my appreciation of others and gratefulness for life.

    1   2   3   4   5

2. As I receive God's love and forgiveness, I find it is easier to accept and forgive myself.

    1   2   3   4   5

3. I am growing in my ability to listen to God in sermons, scripture, and my life.

    1   2   3   4   5

My relationships with others:

4. I am living in love and peace with others as far as it is within my power.

    1   2   3   4   5

5. I contribute to the needs of the poor and powerless or abused so that justice is done in the world.

    1   2   3   4   5

6. I am growing in my ability to cherish people who are different from me and to find the image of God in them.

    1   2   3   4   5

My practice of prayer or inventory:

7. I have a regular practice of prayer—listening to God and noticing where God is active in my life.

    1   2   3   4   5

8. I have a person or group I meet with. Here I can be honest and share my struggles, including those of my spiritual life.

    1   2   3   4   5

Part 3

What questions would you like to discuss or get help with?

CHAPTER 13

Spiritual Formation in Groups

How do you respond when someone asks how the group went or how the church is faring? Do you respond by relating how members of the group "feel" or by quoting statistics? What if we were to ask the question biblically: What fruits of the Spirit are evident?

And how can we encourage these fruits that God is trying to produce in groups? To answer these questions I offer six brief bits of systems theory combined with Christian spirituality. Each includes a question for discernment and evaluation.

At the end of this chapter I give a "Simple Group Discernment" handout you might use with any group. It helps the group work together to discern the direction in which God is leading.

Rooted in Love

For the group to operate well, the leader needs to be rooted and grounded in love, in God—centered, not dependent on the group for identity.

How is *your* anxiety? Can you let go, and let God?

Leadership

For the Christian, Christ is the head. The leader and the group need to listen to Christ in scripture, in the group, in the awareness of each individual.

An effective leader will help the whole group pay attention to what is going on and articulate a vision. Leaders throughout scripture have given a vision of God's hand at work in the community. This is spiritual leadership's first requirement.

I preach regularly on my viewpoint of the parish and remind the group of our common vision or purpose. Yet when I hear parishioners say things that show more discernment than I have, I reflect on these views. When I don't understand or see what is going on, I ask. I remember learning from psychotic patients that one could help me interpret another. As a group we evaluate our performance together on the basis of our vision statement and as we discern what Christ is saying to us.

Do you have a vision? Can you see what is going on? Can you help the group grasp a vision for where the group is going?

Process

Look at the process more than the content. Some psychiatrists call this listening with the third ear. Listen for more than the facts. Listen for the feelings. Listen for what is happening to the group. Look at the result.

When Jesus said, "Not everyone who says, 'Lord, Lord,' will enter the kingdom of heaven, but only the one who does the will of my Father in heaven" (Matt. 7:21), he taught that actions were more important than language.

When I took down some old pictures in our Sunday school wing, I felt justified artistically and theologically. But one of our leaders was furious. I was chagrined, because other changes had been unchallenged: moving the communion table, preaching from a different place in the sanctuary, and having new vestments. I apologized, wondering why old pictures were so important. Why? Because they were given in memory of loved ones. Sacred memories. That was important to many of the older leaders. So we talked about what could be done. We negotiated that there could be a rotation of pictures and some new ones could be put up.

Covey says that the leader needs to try to go for win-win rather than win-lose situations. We must seek to understand rather than be understood.

Have you noticed process more than content?

Work Smart, Not Hard

Don't work too hard and do someone else's job. If a parent does everything for a child, the child learns to be passive and doesn't fend for him–
or herself. It is not helpful for a leader to do everything for a group.
This is not an invitation to passivity but to empowering the members of
the group—which is harder than doing the job yourself.

Jesus spent whole nights in prayer apart from the disciples. When
was the last time you stepped away from your responsibilities to pray?
Moses learned from his father-in-law to delegate. Who helps you see
your blind spots? In a group, I often ask the whole group to evaluate our
process.

Are you trying too hard? Have you asked others to discern with
you?

Change or Growth

For groups going through transition, I point out three words from the
theory of Robert Kegan, who has written extensively about personal
transitions.

Confirm: Affirm that people are where they are supposed to be now;
establish trust. Be responsible and dependable. Affirm people in their
unique gifts. Affirm the history of the group.

Contradict: Give other options about how a project might be seen,
how God might be revealed, about how the group or people might look at
something. God has many points to view. Encourage people to share
their perspective ("I think," "I believe") without attacking the others as
being wrong.

Continuity: Help people worship, be in touch with history, see one's
vision or mission. Help people become more aware of the processes,
internalizing the parish vision and God's purpose.

What is needed now for this group?

Roles

A translation of the Tao—ancient Chinese wisdom—sums up the changing role of the leader:

> A leader must be proactive and do things, intervene, have a vision, keep boundaries clear.
> A leader must be receptive, understanding, and nourish gentleness.
> A leader must withdraw and be still and know that God is God.

Knowing when to do what is a gift of grace, wisdom from above. It cannot be learned by rote. The same role is not always appropriate. It is grace and discipline, skill and instinct. Getting feedback from the group itself helps, although the group at the time may not be the best judge. God is both guide and judge. The leader must ask for guidance and for evaluation.

Where is the call of God to me, to us, now? Have you asked? Have you listened?

Conclusion

I end this book with a description of ministry by Paul: "We are guides into God's most sublime secrets, not security guards posted to protect them" (1 Cor. 4:2 TM). This is often translated "stewards of the mysteries of God." The mystery is not the secrets of the mystery religions, a secret given only to the inner ring of a few; it is the purpose of God from eternity. This is available to everyone who will ask for the gift "to wake up." Colossians 1:27 calls the mystery "Christ in you, the hope of glory." The mystery is the wonder of God's presence inside and outside, transforming individual hearts and history.

And we, pastors and group leaders and friends, are to be guides—like tour guides helping people to open their eyes and see the wonder and glory. We are not only to pay attention to the wonder ourselves, but also to know how to help others. This involves knowing their abilities, nature, limitations, and where they might be most open. Likewise, pastors and small–group leaders must pay attention to the group atmosphere. Unlike a sightseeing tour, the wonders here are found in relationships

and within beings. The appreciation of the wonders and glory are en-
hanced when the whole community is awake to God individually and
together.

This skill or heavenly wisdom we cannot learn in seminary or from
books.

> We didn't learn this by reading books or going to school; we learned
> it from God, who taught us person-to-person through Jesus, and
> we're passing it on to you in the same firsthand, personal way
> (1 Cor. 2:13 TM).

Whatever we do can have this quality. I pray that the Spirit will wake
you more fully for the sake of those around you.

Simple Group Discernment

"Give your entire attention to what God is doing right now"
(Matt. 6:33 TM).

We are to pay attention to what God is doing right now. And that attitude is a gift we can pray for.

1. Start with prayer or prayerful silence.

2. What happened? Were we connected, listening? Did we do what we intended?

3. Where was the activity of the Spirit evident? Did you notice anything that seemed helpful or meaningful? What?

4. How can we improve? What did we not do that we would like to do? What did we do that was not helpful? How can we better align ourselves with our mission or God's dream for us? Where did the formal structure get in the way of the Spirit?

5. End with a prayer or prayerful silence.

NOTES

Introduction

1. Eugene H. Peterson, *Under the Unpredictable Plant* (Grand Rapids: Eerdmans, 1992), 175.

2. Katherine Marie Dyckman and Patrick Carroll, *Inviting the Mystic, Supporting the Prophet* (New York: Paulist, 1981), 18.

Part 1

1. George A. Aschenbrenner, "Consciousness Examen" in *Notes on the Spiritual Exercises of Loyola* (St. Louis: Review for Religious, 1983), 184.

2. Stephen Mitchell, *A Book of Psalms* (New York: Harper Collins, 1993), 33.

Chapter 1

1. Frederick Buechner, *Listening to Your Life* (San Francisco, Harper, 1992), 2.

2. Samuel H. Miller, *The Life of the Soul* (Waco, Tex.: Word Books, 1951), 87.

Chapter 2

1. R. D. Laing, *The Politics of Experience* (New York: Random House, Pantheon Books, 1967), 100-101.

Chapter 3

1. Samuel H. Miller, *The Life of the Soul* (Waco, Tex.: Word Books, 1951), 21.
2. Dom John Chapman, *The Spiritual Letters of Dom John Chapman, O.S.B.* (London: Sheed and Ward, 1946).

Chapter 4

1. Gerald May, *The Awakened Heart* (San Francisco: Harper & Row, 1991), 136.
2. Elizabeth O'Connor, *Our Many Selves* (New York: Harper & Row, 1971), xviii.
3. Ibid., xix.
4. Jean Pierre Camus, quoted in Aldous Huxley, *The Perennial Philosophy* (New York: Harper & Row, 1944), 293.
5. Stephen Covey, *The Seven Habits of Highly Effective People* (New York: Simon & Schuster, 1990).

Chapter 5

1. Evelyn Underhill, *Concerning the Inner Life* (London: Methuen, 1926), 20.
2. Ibid., 53.

Chapter 7

1. Elie Wiesel, *Messengers of God: Biblical Portraits and Legends* (New York: Random House, 1976), 32.
2. Jean Pierre Camus, quoted in Aldous Huxley, *The Perennial Philosophy* (New York: Harper & Row, 1944), 293.

Part 2

1. Gerald May, *Care of Mind, Care of Spirit* (San Francisco: Harper & Row, 1982), 6ff.

Chapter 8

1. Paul Tillich, *The New Being* (New York: Scribner's, 1955), 138.
2. David Steindl-Rast, *Gratefulness, the Heart of Prayer* (New York: Paulist, 1984), 211.
3. Walter Wink, *Engaging the Powers* (Minneapolis: Augsburg, 1993).
4. The Church of the Province of New Zealand, *A New Zealand Prayer Book* (London: Collins, 1989).
5. C. S. Lewis, *Mere Christianity* (New York: Macmillan, 1952), 152.
6. Eugene H. Peterson, *Working the Angles* (Grand Rapids: Eerdmans, 1987), 1, 2.
7. Eugene H. Peterson, *Under the Unpredictable Plant* (Grand Rapids: Eerdmans, 1992), 4.
8. Ibid., 175.
9. Tillich, The New Being, 109.

Chapter 9

1. Frederick Buechner, *Telling Secrets* (San Francisco: Harper & Row, 1991), 193.
2. Edwin H. Friedman, *Generation to Generation* (New York: Guilford Press, 1985), 232– 33.
3. Stephen Covey, *Principle–Centered Leadership* (New York: Simon & Schuster, 1991), 66.
4. Helen Luke, Dark Wood to White Rose: *A Study of Meanings in Dante's Divine Comedy* (Pecos, N.M.: Dove, 1975), 39.

Chapter 10

1. Evelyn Underhill, *Concerning the Inner Life* (London: Methuen, 1926), 14, 15.
2. Robert Kegan, *The Evolving Self* (Cambridge, Mass.: Harvard University Press, 1982).
3. Sam Keen, *The Passionate Life: Stages of Loving* (New York: Harper & Row, 1983).

Chapter 11

1. Evelyn Underhill, *Concerning the Inner Life* (London: Methuen, 1926), 54. Emphasis mine.
2. Ibid., 35, 36.
3. C. S. Lewis, *Till We Have Faces* (Grand Rapids: Eerdmans, 1956), 294.

BIBLIOGRAPHY

Bible

Peterson, Eugene. *The Message: The New Testament in Contemporary Language.* Colorado Springs: NavPress, 1993.

For the Beginning Again Course

Buechner, Frederick. *Listening to Your Life.* San Francisco: Harper, 1992.
Hybels, Bill. *Too Busy Not to Pray.* Downers Grove, Ill.: InterVarsity Press, 1988.
Roth, Nancy. *The Breath of God.* Cambridge, Mass.: Cowley, 1990.
Steindl–Rast, David. *Gratefulness, the Heart of Prayer.* Ramsey, N.J.: Paulist Press, 1984.

Personality and Temperament

Ackerman, John. *Finding Your Way: Personalized Practices for Spiritual Growth through the Myers–Briggs Type Indicator.* Washington, D.C.: The Alban Institute, 1992.
Bridges, William. *The Character of Organizations: Using Jungian Type in Organizational Development.* Palo Alto, Calif.: Consulting Psychologists Press, 1992.
Edwards, Lloyd. *How We Belong, Fight, and Pray: The MBTI as a*

Key to Congregational Dynamics. Washington, D.C.: The Alban
    Institute, 1993.
Giovannoni, Louise, Linda V. Berens, and Sue A. Cooper. *Introduc-
    tion to Temperament.* Huntington Beach, Calif.: Telos Publica-
    tions, 1987. Can be ordered direct from Temperament Research
    Institute, 16152 Beach Blvd., Suite 117, Huntington Beach, CA
    92647.
Isachsen, Olaf, and Linda V. Berens. *Working Together: A Personal-
    ity Centered Approach to Management.* Coronado, Calif.:
    Neworld Management Press, 1988.
Oswald, Roy, and Otto Kroger. *Personality Type and Religious
    Leadership.* Washington, D.C.: The Alban Institute, 1988.

Adult Stages of Development

Keen, Sam. *The Passionate Life: Stages of Loving.* New York: Harper
    & Row, 1983.
Kegan, Robert. *The Evolving Self: Problem and Process in Human
    Development.* Cambridge, Mass.: Harvard University Press,
    1982.
Leibert, Elizabeth. *Changing Life Patterns: Adult Development in
    Spiritual Direction.* New York: Paulist Press, 1992.
Parks, Sharon. *The Critical Years: Young Adults and the Search for
    Meaning, Faith, and Commitment.* San Francisco: Harper &
    Row, 1985.

Male–Female

Pierce, Carol, and Bill Page. *A Male/Female Continuum: Paths to
    Colleagueship.* Laconia, N.H.: New Dynamics, 1986.
Gilligan, Carol. *In a Different Voice.* Cambridge, Mass.: Harvard
    University Press, 1982.
Ocherson, Samuel. *Finding Our Fathers: How a Man's Life Is
    Shaped by His Relationship with His Father.* New York: Fawcett
    Columbine, 1986.
Hahn, Celia Allison. *Sexual Paradox: Creative Tensions in Our Lives
    and in Our Congregations.* New York: Pilgrim Press, 1991.

Spirituality

Anonymous. *A Healing Journey*. Center City, Minn.: Hazelden, 1986.

Barry, William, and William J. Connolly. *The Practice of Spiritual Direction*. New York: Seabury Press, 1982.

Borg, Marcus. *Jesus, a New Vision: Spirit, Culture, and the Life of Discipleship*. San Francisco: Harper & Row, 1987.

Covey, Robert. *The Seven Habits of Highly Effective People*. New York: Simon and Schuster, 1989.

Huggett, Joyce. *The Joy of Listening to God*. Downers Grove, Ill.: InterVarsity Press, 1986.

Edwards, Tilden. *Living in the Presence*. San Francisco: Harper & Row, 1987.

May, Gerald G. *Care of Mind/Care of Spirit*. San Francisco: Harper & Row, 1982.

Norris, Kathleen. *Dakota: A Spiritual Geography*. New York: Tickman and Fields, 1993.

Fitzpatrick, Jean Grasso. *Something More: Nurturing Your Children's Spiritual Growth*. New York: Penguin, 1991.

Hendrix, Harville. *Getting the Love You Want: A Guide for Couples*. San Francisco: Harper & Row, 1988.

Larkin, Ernest. *Silent Presence: Discernment as Process and Problem*. Denville, N.J.: Dimension, 1981.

Kurtz, Ernest. *Shame and Guilt: Characteristics of the Dependency Cycle*. Center City, Minn.: Hazelden, 1981.

Tugwell, Simon. *Ways of Imperfection: An Exploration of Christian Spirituality*. Springfield, Ill.: Templegate, 1985.

Underhill, Evelyn. *Concerning the Inner Life*. London: Methuen, 1926.

Spirituality for Leaders

Guenther, Margaret. *Holy Listening; The Art of Spiritual Direction*. Cambridge, Mass.: Cowley, 1992.

Hart, Thomas N. *The Art of Christian Listening*. New York: Paulist Press, 1980.

Peterson, Eugene. *Under the Unpredictable Plant: An Exploration in Vocational Holiness*. Grand Rapids: Eerdmans, 1992.

_____. *Working the Angles: The Shape of Pastoral Integrity.* Grand Rapids: Eerdmans, 1987.

The Alban Institute:
an invitation to membership

The Alban Institute, begun in 1979, believes that the congregation is essential to the task of equipping the people of God to minister in the church and the world. A multi-denominational membership organization, the Institute provides on-site training, educational programs, consulting, research, and publishing for hundreds of churches across the country.

The Alban Institute invites you to be a member of this partnership of laity, clergy, and executives—a partnership that brings together people who are raising important questions about congregational life and people who are trying new solutions, making new discoveries, finding a new way of getting clear about the task of ministry. The Institute exists to provide you with the kinds of information and resources you need to support your ministries.

Join us now and enjoy these benefits:

CONGREGATIONS: The Alban Journal, a highly respected journal published six times a year, to keep you up to date on current issues and trends.

Inside Information, Alban's quarterly newsletter, keeps you informed about research and other happenings around Alban. Available to members only.

Publications Discounts:

- ☐ 15% for Individual, Retired Clergy, and Seminarian Members
- ☐ 25% for Congregational Members
- ☐ 40% for Judicatory and Seminary Executive Members

Discounts on Training and Education Events

Write our Membership Department at the address below or call us at 1-800-486-1318 or 301-718-4407 for more information about how to join The Alban Institute's growing membership, particularly about Congregational Membership in which 12 designated persons receive all benefits of membership.

The Alban Institute, Inc.
Suite 433 North
4550 Montgomery Avenue
Bethesda, MD 20814-3341